OUTLAW WOMEN

OUTLAW WOMEN

America's Most Notorious Daughters,
Wives, and Mothers

ROBERT BARR SMITH

TWODOT®

GUILFORD, CONNECTICUT
HELENA, MONTANA

A · TWODOT® · BOOK

An imprint and registered trademark of Rowman & Littlefield

Distributed by NATIONAL BOOK NETWORK

British Library Cataloguing-in-Publication Information available

Library of Congress Cataloging-in-Publication Data

Smith, Robert B. (Robert Barr), 1933-
  Outlaw women : the Wild West's most notorious daughters, wives, and mothers / Robert Barr Smith.
    pages cm
  Includes bibliographical references and index.
  ISBN 978-1-4422-4729-1 (paperback : alkaline paper) -- ISBN 978-1-4422-4730-7 (e-book)
  1. Women outlaws--West (U.S.)--Biography. 2. Female offenders--West (U.S.)--Biography. 3. Women--West (U.S.)--Biography. 4. Crime--West (U.S.)--History. 5. Frontier and pioneer life--West (U.S.) 6. West (U.S.)--Biography. 7. West (U.S.)--Social conditions. I. Title.
  F590.5.S65 2015
  364.1092'520978--dc23
                            2015016897

♾™ The paper used in this publication meets the minimum requirements of American National Standard for Information Sciences—Permanence of Paper for Printed Library Materials, ANSI/NISO Z39.48-1992.

CONTENTS

Foreword

Americans have always had a soft spot in their hearts for the dashing lady criminals, particularly those who galloped across the broad stage of the western United States with their outlaw lovers. Or are supposed to have done so.

Sadly, many of the popular heroines of American crime aren't quite as tough as some tales make them out to be, especially those who graced the western part of our young, growing nation. Their image—their "history," if that's the word—has been the stuff of much storytelling, much exaggeration, and a lot of downright creative mythology.

After all, most readers in our bumptious, burly, brawling young nation were excited about all the deeds of derring-do they heard about, and hungry for more. Since there was never enough of the real stuff to go around, satisfying the public required the invention of lot of deeds and dialogue, and even of places and people. The rule for many old-time writers about such things—and even some not so old-time—often was, well, it might have happened that way, or well, there could have been somebody like that. And thus was born some of what passes for modern-day "history," invention masquerading as fact. If most of it is vastly entertaining, not all of it is what old-timers would call the "gospel truth."

Virtually all of the women who march through popular history had about them some element of flamboyance, some contempt for the morals and mores of their day. Some were corrupt; some were brutal, even murderous; all were liars to some degree, or at least exaggerators of real ability; many were courageous and some were downright brilliant.

All were marvelously entertaining.

Take Joyce Turner. Joyce didn't like her husband Alonzo much, which was nothing unusual for a lot of wives, then and later. But Joyce, egged on by a couple of girlfriends during an evening kaffeklatch, put her dislike of Alonzo to lethal action. With a friend's words ringing in her ears, "Well, are you going to do it, or not?," she went home and did indeed do it, fatally shooting Alonzo while he slept.

Joyce showed no sign of repentance, even after listening to the judge hand her a life sentence. As she told reporters, "Alonzo always told me that he wanted to die in bed. I simply arranged for it." Even if Joyce broke the law, you still have to admire her panache, and her way with words.

In the case of Martha Wise, the motive for murder seems to have been nothing more than pure pride. Martha was a lonely, plain widow, just getting by on a hardscrabble farm in Ohio in the 1920s. Martha conceived a passion for a much younger man called Walter Johns. Her mother and her uncle and aunt—Fred and Lily Gienke—made fun of her passion, which after all was nobody's business but Martha's. Martha reacted.

Martha's mother was the first irritation to vanish; the old lady was fed a lethal dose of arsenic by her loving daughter on the first day of January 1925. Aunt and uncle passed into the Great Beyond the next month, also on the wings of arsenic, and others of the Gienke family became ill but recovered. Once arsenic was found in the bodies of all the dead, suspicion naturally fell on Martha.

Under persistent questioning, Martha admitted it. "Yes, I did it," she said, "but it was the devil made me do it." And while she was at it, she also confessed to a series of burglaries and arsons: "I like fires. They were red and bright, and I loved to see the flames shooting up into the sky."

Her trial was a sensation. Although Martha was tried in the newspapers as the "the Borgia of America," her defense team was still adept enough that she managed to avoid the death penalty. The turning point may have been the testimony of her lover, Johns, who said, among other things, that during their love-making sessions Martha "barked like a dog." Whether that was the truth or a bit of boasting by Johns about his own ability in bed, it saved Martha's bacon. The sentence was life.

Some of the other ladies who get chapters in this book committed their crimes alone; some had help. All were probably as famous as their time Martha and Joyce; some were even more so, especially those of surpassing evil like Belle Gunness; but even those who were vastly overrated left some footprints in the sands of time.

Let us rejoice in the certainty that they will not return.

CHAPTER ONE

A Legend in Her Own Mind

Belle Starr

I was just a lad in the "good old days" of the silver screen. Television was only a fanciful idea back then, movies were cheap—especially if you were a kid—and a big bag of popcorn cost only a nickel. Invariably—at least in Saturday matinees—you got to watch a double feature, plus an installment or two of *Buck Rogers*, a newsreel, the previews, the Road Runner outwitting Wile E. Coyote—maybe even two of those—the ads for the car dealer, and the plumber, and whoever else you might need locally. You got a whole lot of entertainment for thirty cents, and you got to sit with your friends.

One end of the double feature was sure to be a western, sometimes both if you were lucky. That's where my buddies and I learned all about the history of the Old West, or at least we thought we did. We figured the singing cowboys—Gene Autry and his like—were probably phony; but the others looked real. We learned a lot of history—we thought—from the heroics of Lash Larue, Randolph Scott and other straight shooters of that ilk. Youthful dreams don't pass away easily, and it took me a lot of years to learn that most of what I saw in the theater was entertaining hogwash.

Take for instance the inevitable Main Street gunfight, a fixture of the westerns of those days. We watched fascinated as two men swaggered toward each other, hands poised claw-like above their holstered Colts—sometimes two of them. Then, when the gunfighters were almost nose to nose, one of them said something moronic, like, "This town ain't big enough for both of us," and the two dug for their revolvers and fired point-blank. The guy in the white hat always won.

Belle Starr

Our youthful minds were not encumbered by any knowledge of the real Code of the Gunfighter. *Don't take chances. Don't face your enemy, for Pete's sake; shoot him in the back. Shoot him in the back in the dark if possible. Don't give him even half a chance to get off a shot. It's safer that way.*

One of my most precious early movie memories was of Belle Starr, played by Gene Tierney, I think, who was by any standard one of the loveliest women ever to appear in film. In our young minds, Gene was Belle Starr, the Bandit Queen, the daring leader of a daring gang, galloping about the countryside without, of course, a hair out of place. Back in the 1940s I discovered Belle/Gene, and I think I fell in love on the spot.

Disillusionment was a while in coming, but as I got older I began to read more than comic books and found out what Belle was *really* like. Another treasured illusion was gone forever, and one of the best of them. For as I sadly discovered, Belle was hardly the Bandit Queen. On her best days she was a small-time horse thief, a sort of criminal moll who cast a long shadow with very little substance behind it, a little like the wizard in *The Wizard of Oz.*

She was no rival to Gene Tierney to start with, and as the years went by, she gradually became a truly ugly harridan, the kind of woman westerners would say had been "rid hard and put away wet." So much for the queen part.

Still, she belongs in this book, since her legend is far too solidly established to ever pass away. And in fact she had much to do with real outlaws in her time, not least of whom was her father-in-law, the formidable Old Tom Starr. And she married a couple of other outlaws too, both of whom died of terminal lead poisoning.

And, according to legend, Belle dallied with an assortment of other hardcases along the way. That includes Cole Younger, who, western legend says, fathered her daughter Pearl, something Cole denied to his dying day. And in this, at least, Cole was probably telling the truth.

Belle has probably inspired more claptrap than any other outlaw in the history of the West, which is saying rather a lot. Part of the legend says Belle was Cherokee (she wasn't), that she had Cole Younger's child (no, she didn't), that she galloped about carrying messages for Missouri guerrillas during the Civil War (probably not).

Some of the florid prose written about her reached epic proportions. Take this extraordinary nonsense written by somebody who called himself Captain Kit Dalton: "A more winning smile never illumined the face of a Madonna; a more cruel human never walked the deck of a pirate ship . . . this phenomenally beautiful half savage . . . a maroon Diana in the chase, a Venus in beauty, a Minerva in Wisdom."

What a woman! What a criminal mastermind! What a load of horsefeathers!

Another similar bit of extraordinary hyperbole appeared in something called *Remarkable Rogues: The Careers of Some Notable Criminals in Europe and America (Kingston 1921)*. This fairy tale excites the reader with the revelation that at fifteen Belle killed her first man, a camp robber, strangling him "with her small white hands." Sure she did.

In S. W. Harman's *Hell on the Border (1992)*, Belle is a finished and ruthless outlaw, a sort of super-bandit: "Of all the noted women ever mentioned by word or pen, none have been more brilliantly daring nor more effective in their chosen roles than Belle Starr, champion and leader of robbers; herself a sure shot and a murderess."

That was the most obvious twaddle, but long years later, even some of the old-timers in Indian Territory told fanciful tales of Belle. One of them went like this: "I remember one time the law was after Belle and she stopped at a negro cabin; she made the negro woman hide her. She dressed up in a black dress with a white apron and shawl, blacked her face, and when the law came in she was rocking in a chair with a cob pipe in her mouth."

Why shore, folks. That fable, like the others, is about as believable as one of the tales of Mother Goose, but it was only one of the many bizarre stories told of the Bandit Queen. In fact, the truth is at once stranger and more prosaic.

Belle was a Missouri girl, born plain old Myra Maybelle Shirley on a farm up near Carthage, Missouri. That was in 1848, and Belle's father was a successful man in that year, and a slaveholder. Myra Maybelle—if a picture purporting to be the lass in fact is her—was quite attractive in those far-off days. Then came the horrors of the Civil War, casting their long ugly shadow across the land, and all of the peaceful life changed.

The family was living in Carthage then, where Myra Maybelle got an education at the Carthage Female Academy. The stories about her tell that she received an excellent education for the time, as most girls did not, and also became an accomplished musician. Her father was still prospering, now in the inn-keeping business, but the war would largely ruin him, as it destroyed so many others.

His eldest son, Bud, joined a band of Missouri guerrillas, Bushwhackers, and was killed, and in time the town of Carthage was burned. There are all sorts of stories about young Belle's heroics during the war, "fired to deeds of valor" by "her hot Southern blood," as one sensational writer put it. Legend has Belle galloping about the countryside carrying messages for her brother's guerrilla band, or even acting as a spy. She was "frequently with Cole Younger and the James boys," the story goes, even though the Younger brothers and the James boys rode with different guerrilla units.

With Bud's death and the loss of much of his property, the senior Shirley had enough of the vicious border war and moved his family south, settling near Scyene, Texas, now a part of Dallas. Belle grew to womanhood there, and in 1866 married a hoodlum called Jim Reed, who was then already on the run from the law.

Two years later a daughter appeared and was officially named Rosie; Belle called her "her pearl," however, and Pearl she remained for the rest of her days. Pearl would grow up to a sort of eminence in the harlot trade as both prostitute and madam, but that was a long way in the future. The Reeds lived for a time in the sanctuary of Old Tom Starr's spread down on the Canadian River in Indian Territory, but in 1871 they were living in California, where their son Ed was born. Reed was a professional criminal, and by this time was wanted for murder. There are tales that Belle was his confederate in crime, at least to the point of fencing horses her husband had stolen. The legends about her robbing and murdering—which have no solid foundation—are probably no more than a part of the mythology surrounding Belle's life.

A major source of the undying myth about Belle and her "gang" is Harman's *Hell on the Border,* the rousing book purporting to be a history of the formidable Judge Parker's court at Fort Smith. Belle, Harman says, collected a set of "admirers as reckless as herself," each becoming her lover, according to Harman, *seriatim*. These adoring desperados, according to Harman, included Jim French, Jack Spaniard, and Blue Duck, all truly nasty pieces of work in fact. These hardcases "[s]tood ready to obey the woman they admired yet feared, who could out ride, out jump, and out shoot them all, who could draw her pistol from its convenient holster at her side in a twinkling and who never missed a mark." And a lot more purple prose of the same kind. *Hell on the Border* may be a mine of misinformation, but it sure is entertaining.

Two 1874 incidents are probably the best known of her so-called outlaw career. The first was the robbery of the San Antonio–Austin stage coach. There is no real evidence that Belle had anything to do with the crime, let alone that she was a part of the holdup itself. The second crime in which Belle is supposed to have had a part was the robbery of a wealthy Indian of a purported $30,000.

That was an especially ugly incident. The victim, Watt Grayson, at first refused to tell Reed and two other bandits where he kept his cash. And so they then threw a noose around Grayson's neck and hoisted him clear of the ground until he nearly strangled. When this cruelty produced no result, his tormentors turned on Grayson's wife and began the same torture. Grayson was plenty tough, but he would not let his wife suffer, and so the bandits got their money. Once more, there is no evidence that Belle was even present, although her husband Jim Reed probably was part of the robber gang.

Reed lasted until the summer of 1874, when he came in second in a gunfight with a deputy in Paris, Texas. There is a charming tale that Belle refused to identify what was left of Reed in order to deny the officer the reward carried on Reed's head. Nice story, but again without foundation.

Belle was now a widow, but she would not remain that way for long. She is said to have dallied with Bruce Younger up in southern Kansas, maybe even marrying him, but whatever the relationship was, if any, it did not last. And then, in the summer of 1880, she married Sam Starr down in the Cherokee Nation. Sam was the son of Old Tom Starr, one of the really ferocious fighting men of the Territory, and the couple settled on his property.

Somewhere along the way the place began to be called Younger's Bend, which spawned still another legend: that Belle named the place, still carrying a torch for Cole Younger, according to legend the father of her Pearl. This seems to be no more than still another folk myth, for the place was named Younger's Bend by Old Tom himself, who apparently had some admiration for the Missouri outlaw.

In 1883, Belle and her new husband did a short stretch at the Detroit House of Correction for horse stealing, but when their time was up they returned to Younger's Bend. And then, in 1886, Sam Starr was attending a dance when he ran into a hated adversary, one Frank West. The two wasted no time in reaching for their guns, and in a few minutes both men were dead. Belle was once more a widow.

Here the mists of mythology close in again. Belle was moved to continue her budding career as bedfellow to various disreputable outlaw types, although it's not entirely clear who all her lovers might have been. She is quoted as having said, "I am a friend to any brave and gallant outlaw."

Sure enough. She was more than a friend to a whole passel of outlaws, if legend is anywhere near accurate. A host of stories have her cavorting with a veritable galaxy of luminaries in the outlaw world, including—at least—Jack Spaniard, Jim French, Jim July (who ended up answering to the handle of Jim Starr), and a man much younger than the now-aging Belle, one Blue Duck.

Although Belle was no longer a ravishing beauty—if she ever was—she seems to have carried on with her bed-hopping career, albeit she had become, as one source neatly put it, "bony and flat-chested, with a mean mouth." She also continued to indulge in her second passion for having her picture taken *a la outlaw*, holding at least one gun and sometimes posed on a very tall horse.

Whatever carnal delights Belle may have indulged in, she also paid attention to her home at Younger's Bend. And that was probably what ended her life prematurely. For she had at least one sharecropper tenant, a thoroughly worthless man called Ed Watson. He had come out of Arkansas, but was originally from Florida, where he was wanted for murder, among other things. Belle seems to have found out about Ed's nasty past . . . and it was a little too much knowledge for continued good health.

Blue Duck and Belle Starr

Belle and Watson got into a dispute when Belle, afraid of more trouble with the authorities if she were discovered harboring a fugitive, told Watson to leave her land and sent him a letter returning his rent money. The two argued, and Belle incautiously told the man that while federal marshals might not be interested in him, "the Florida officers might." It was not a wise thing to say.

Although others were suspected as her killers then and afterward—including her own son—it seems pretty clear that a furious Watson decided to close Belle's mouth forever about his dirty career in Florida. Either he or somebody else waylaid her and blew her out of the saddle with a shotgun. And so, in February of 1889 Belle passed to her reward, whatever that might be. She was buried at Younger's Bend—with a revolver in her hand, according to a legend. The myth was off to a good start.

Watson was charged but never tried. There simply was not enough evidence against him to take to court. But knowing that Jim July Starr would almost certainly try to kill him, Watson left the state and at last ended up back in Florida, where he went on killing, running up a tally of as many as ten or twelve people. In time he ran afoul of some tough peace officers who filled him full of holes.

As for Belle's "Pearl," she carried on with her prostitute/madam career. Finally exiled from Fort Smith after repeated arrests, she drifted west, dying in an Arizona hotel in the summer of 1925.

In December of 1896, Belle's son Ed Reed got full of tarantula juice in a saloon run by a man named Tom Clark. Reed got rowdy, "brandishing his six shooter in a very careless way and abusing the bystanders and shooting up the place generally" as the Muskogee *Phoenix* put it. Clark was understandably upset, and some hard words passed between the men. Reed left, but came back with a Winchester and threatened Clark. It turned out to be a bad idea, for Clark was quicker and shot Reed twice, whereof he expired.

It was as well that Belle was not around to see the end of her children, but she sure would have enjoyed Gene Tierney's sterling performance.

CHAPTER TWO

Black Widow

Belle Gunness

For two excellent reasons Belle Gunness stands out among the many Norwegian immigrants who helped build America. First, she was an amazon, particularly for her day: she was tall and weighed well over two hundred pounds. Second, she was totally without anything resembling a conscience, quintessentially evil.

Both of these qualities, plus extraordinary physical strength, made her eminently well qualified for her life's work: killing people. Belle wasn't particular about whom she murdered: mostly she killed for profit; sometimes she killed to eliminate possible witnesses, to tidy up, as it were. Before she was through she had murdered at least forty people, including a goodly number of her own relatives.

She was born Brynhild Paulsdatter Stòrseth in the town of Selbu, some sixty kilometers from the city of Trondheim, probably in 1859. She grew up in poverty, took domestic service for three years or so, and by 1888 had earned enough to come to America. Maybe by way of apologia, there is a tale that while still in Norway she had been attacked by a man who kicked her in the stomach, causing her to lose a child. Thereafter, the story goes, "her personality changed markedly."

Perhaps that helps account for the vile things Belle would do in the new world, or perhaps the tale is only a well-meaning attempt to explain what she did later. Before she left Norway, it is said, the man who had attacked her died of stomach cancer. Maybe so, maybe not; in hindsight, considering Belle's future doings, the man's death is clouded with some suspicion.

Belle Gunness

Reaching Chicago, she married Mads Sorensen. The two opened a confectionary store, but the venture was unsuccessful, or at least it was until the shop burned down and the insurance was paid. The cause was said to be an "exploding kerosene lamp," although no lamp was found in the burned-out ruins. The insurance money paid for a suburban home that soon also burned, producing a fresh infusion of insurance money; that paid for still another home. At least by this time, Belle must have had a clear concept of the value of insurance.

It is unclear how many children Belle had, and by whom, but there is evidence that Belle and Mads had four, two of whom died in infancy of "acute colitis," which could be a number of ailments, including acute poisoning. An adopted child, Jennie, was also part of the household at this time.

Husband Mads was the next to go, oddly on the only day on which two policies on his life were both in force. A coincidence, of course, although some of his relations thought the diagnosis of "heart failure" was less likely than an overdose of arsenic. On the day after his funeral Belle applied for the insurance, a payout totaling $8,500, a goodly pot of money for the time.

Belle invested next in a palatial house in La Porte, Indiana, an older home complete with carriage house, pier, boathouse and pungent history, for it had once been a high-class bordello. After Belle bought the home in 1891, both boat house and carriage house burned to the ground—insured, of course.

The next year, Belle married again, this time to Peter Gunness, a butcher. Just a week later, Peter's baby daughter died while she was alone with Belle, and before the year was out Peter followed her when, according to Belle, part of a sausage machine fell from a shelf and split his head open. Lots of people doubted that dubious cause, including the coroner, but a coroner's jury disagreed.

Fourteen-year-old Jennie was called before the jury and asked about a statement she made to a classmate: "My momma killed my papa. She hit him with a meat cleaver and he died. Don't tell a soul." Jennie denied she said it, and the whole ugly mess passed into history.

So did Jennie, in 1906. She had gone to a "Lutheran College in Los Angeles," Belle said, or to a "finishing school." In fact, Jennie hadn't gone nearly that far; she would turn up later, in a grave on her adoptive mother's farm.

Belle now began advertising in the newspaper "personals," telling eligible men that she was a "comely widow who owns a large farm . . . desires to make the acquaintance of a gentleman equally well provided, with view of joining fortunes . . . Triflers need not apply." The ad brought on a veritable parade of eligible men, who showed up with lots of cash money to show they were "equally well provided." They came to stay with Belle at her farmhouse, but with one exception, they never left. That lucky man, one Anderson, had wakened in the night to find Belle standing over him, holding a candle and looking so "foreboding and sinister" that he yelled, jumped into his clothes, and caught the first train back to Missouri. He was wise.

Her impassioned letters to potential suitors dripped passion and urgency, with lines like "my heart beats with wild rapture for you." At least one urged the next victim to "come prepared to stay forever." And he did. Underground.

There were suspicions a-plenty around La Porte. For one thing, Belle never opened her shutters day or night, and she had been seen in the darkness digging in her hog pen. She had also ordered a series of big trunks to be delivered to her house, trunks big enough to accommodate a corpse.

All these mysterious activities were suggestive, but nobody had anything that could be acted upon. And so the suitors came—and stayed—courtesy of Belle and, after a while, her "handyman," Ray Lamphere. Lamphere was apparently wildly in love with Belle, in spite of her murderous ways and the fact that whatever went into the ads, a "suitable suitor" was always between him and his light of love. Lamphere must have wondered when he could bury the last suitable suitor in the hog pen and have Belle all to himself.

Instead, Belle tired of Lamphere and his jealous ways, fired him, and then had the temerity to go complaining to the police that he was threatening her. She also whined loudly that he was insane, and actually got him medically examined. The verdict went in favor of sanity although, given Belle's gross appearance and murderous disposition, it would seem that any attachment to her had to demonstrate a streak of madness.

Lamphere wouldn't go away, either, and was heard to say things like "Helgelien won't bother me no more. We fixed him for keeps." Since Andrew Helgelien had appeared as a suitor and then abruptly vanished, that statement must have smelled like danger to Belle.

Especially was this true because Helgelien's brother was concerned about his missing sibling and did not believe Belle's protestations that he was not around La Porte; maybe, she said, he had gone to Norway to visit relatives, a suggestion that the brother did not buy for a moment.

Since the brother said he was coming down to investigate, and Lamphere was a continuing danger, Belle had to act. First, she told her lawyer that Lamphere had threatened to kill her and burn her house down, although she omitted to pass on this frightening notion to the police. She needed a will, she told the lawyer, leaving everything to her children, a macabre statement in view of what happened shortly afterward. Belle then went down to the bank and paid off her mortgage.

She had a new hired hand by then, one Maxon, who awoke in his upstairs room in the house to find the structure wrapped in sheets of flame. Maxon only escaped by jumping from the second story in his underwear, but by the time he could find help the house was a smoking ruin. Inside, as the ruins cooled, searchers found the bodies of three children and a woman. The kids were presumably Belle's, but the dead woman did not seem to fit.

First off, some curiosity was aroused by the fact that the dead woman's body had no head, and no stray head was ever found. The search for it did turn up eight men's watches, however, and an assortment of human teeth. Second, although a dentist identified Belle's dentures as those discovered in the wreckage, the charred corpse didn't look nearly big enough to be the stalwart Belle—no more than 150 pounds compared to Belle's 200-plus. Several people who knew her looked at the body and opined that it wasn't Belle at all.

Lamphere was arrested, however, on the strength of the story of his threats as told by Belle to her attorney. And a young man turned up who said he been "watching the house"—no reason given—and saw Lamphere running away just prior to the fire. The case became further convoluted when an autopsy revealed that the dead woman in the burned-out house was not only headless but full of strychnine.

About this time Helgelien's brother showed up, and complained to the sheriff that his brother had probably met with foul play at Belle's hands. Handyman Maxon volunteered the interesting information that Belle had ordered him to bring many wheelbarrow-loads of dirt into the hog-pen to fill, he was told, depressions where "rubbish" was buried.

That was enough for the Sheriff, who took a dozen men to the farm and began to dig. They hit pay dirt immediately. The more they dug, the worse things got, and by the time they finished the diggers had uncovered a charnel house. The remains of more than forty people had turned up, several of them children, including foster daughter Jennie Olson. A number of the dead remained forever unidentified, but many were named, then or later, as Belle's mail-order suitors.

In Belle's barn were several horses that had once belonged to would-be suitors, and it was conclusively proved that Belle's bridgework—found at the scene of the fire—could not have survived the fierce flames in the pristine state in which it was found. It was hers, all right, but it certainly hadn't been through a fire in the mouth of the corpse. It had obviously been planted, post fire.

And Belle? She was no longer anyplace to be found, and over the following years remained a phantom, vanished as if she never was. For some twenty years, the La Porte sheriff got an average of two sighting reports a month. Although none of them panned out, her monumental murder-for-profit enterprise earned her a sort of dubious fame: she was enshrined in a folk song in 1938, a couple of eminently forgettable movies, and something called a multi-media concert, or play, which appeared in 2009.

At last, in early 1910, much of Belle's vile history was revealed when a clergyman told of a deathbed confession made to him by Lamphere, in prison for the arson of Belle's farm. Lamphere had told the clergyman that he had been an accessory after the fact to many of Belle's murders; he had done the burying, he said; but she had done the killing herself. Her *modus operandi*, he said, went like this:

After a sumptuous dinner, Belle would serve her current victim coffee, drugged, of course; once he had passed out, she got out her meat cleaver and finished the job. For variation, she sometimes waited until the victim went to bed and chloroformed him, or simply spiked his after-dinner coffee with strychnine. The remains were then consigned to the hog pen or sometimes to the hog-scalding vat and a coating of quicklime. Lamphere had even known his beloved to chop up a victim and feed the pieces to her hogs. Waste not, want not.

The headless substitute for Belle herself turned out to be a Chicago woman Belle had pretended to interview as a housekeeper. She smashed this unfortunate in the head, then removed the head and dumped it in the swamp. Her own children were next, chloroformed and smothered. Then came the fire and Belle's disappearance, after she carefully closed out her bank accounts.

Wherever Belle had gone, she was not poor. Her gentle ways with suitors had netted her something in the neighborhood of a quarter of a million dollars, an enormous sum for the time. Belle was someplace comfortable, enjoying her fortune—and maybe adding to it?

CHAPTER THREE

Communing with the Spirits

Kate Bender

When she was good
she was very, very good;
but when she was bad,
she was horrid!

Alfred, Lord Tennyson, had it right. He wasn't describing the lovely Kate Bender, but his words fit her to a T, for in a very tough part of America, and in a whole family of true psychotics, she was a star.

In the years just after the Civil War, the so-called Western Movement accelerated, and hundreds of thousands of people braved strange new lands and hostile Indians, hard trails and danger, looking for the Promised Land.

Many of them were new immigrants, ordinary people looking for a better life, a real future for themselves and their families in this new land of promise. In this wonderful new world a man could settle on a piece of land and make it his own, no landlord, no crop-sharing, no Kaiser, no Czar, no Duke whoever, nobody to tell a man what to do.

It sounds a small thing in our times, but in fact it was a dream come true to hundreds of thousands of eager people. To the waves of pilgrims from the settled East coast of the United States and the hungry newcomers from across the wide ocean, were added many people from the South after the Civil War, leaving a ruined, defeated land for a new start in a free nation.

"Evil Genius" Kate Bender

Imagine 160 acres of your very own just for the "proving-up"; it was a glowing vision to most of the families moving west. To most of the European immigrants, 160 acres of your own was an impossible dream suddenly come true; if it meant days and days of back-breaking work, why, at least what you had when you finished was *yours*.

Most of these people were solid citizens, the salt the western earth was hungry for, willing to work any number of hours in all kinds of weather to build something for themselves, something to have and to hold, something of value to leave their children. Most of them were devout people, people who wanted to live in peace and follow the law, divine and terrestrial. They were the ideal material to build a great nation.

But there were the others. Along with the good, God-fearing people came the criminal scum, not interested in hard work, or for that matter in work of any kind. Many were fugitives from prosecution or from jail in distant parts. What all of them came west for, besides refuge from the law, was a consuming interest in what they could take away from people who worked for it, and sometimes in simply gratifying their own egos by brutalizing others.

But the Bender family was different. Its four members exuded an aura of intense evil not common even in the tough, wild land west of the Mississippi. Their crimes were plain enough, murder and larceny; it was the rest of it that turned other people's stomachs.

The Bender family's lives otherwise remain a profound mystery. In the first place, it is unclear whether they were in fact a family at all. The patriarch was a hulking, unsociable brute of a man—somebody described him as "like a gorilla"; he spoke a guttural, virtually indecipherable variety of what in those days was called *plat Deutsch*, Low German.

Referred to as "beetle-browed John" and otherwise known as Pa Bender, he was perhaps sixty years old. His dumpy wife, inevitably "Ma," was somewhat younger, maybe fifty-five, so unsociable and withdrawn that some folks called her the "she-devil." Ma Bender declared herself to be psychic; she spoke to the spirits, she said, and maybe she thought she did, given what happened later on. One neighbor put it neatly: "We thought Mr. Bender was an ugly cuss, but she's no improvement."

There were two children—or at least they were believed and held out to be children—son John and daughter Kate. John was given to oft-repeated spasms of giggling, which led some people to think, as one author quaintly put it, he was "a few bricks shy of a full load," but Kate was much admired, being called "beautiful" and "voluptuous" among other good things. She was also, it appears, something of a flirt, but she had her darker side, much darker, as will appear.

Like her sullen mother, the lovely Kate also boasted of her prowess in spirit-talking, even devising a handbill calling herself rather grandly, *Professor Miss Katie Bender,* and advertising her ability to "heal all sort of diseases; can cure Blindness, Fits, Deafness . . . also Deaf and Dumbness." She is said to have journeyed to small settlements round about to demonstrate her clairvoyant powers, "curing" the sick and holding séances with a variety of spirits.

In short, the whole family was a spooky lot, save for the much-admired Kate. But then, people lived much farther apart in those pioneer days, and it took longer to get to know even your neighbors at all well.

The family settled on two adjoining homesteads in brand-new Labette County, Kansas. The area was very sparsely peopled when the two male Benders arrived in the autumn of 1870; it had been much fought over by frontier guerrillas, "made perfectly desolate" by the year the Civil War ended. But now eager pilgrims were coming in ever-mounting numbers, and some of the filth of the earth came with them.

Pa and John Jr. settled two adjoining parcels of 160 acres each, one of which was a long, narrow strip running beside the Osage Trail, which led from Independence northeast to St. Paul. It was regularly used by travelers of all kinds; thus its attraction for people eager to set up a little business—or to start committing wholesale murder.

The two Bender men built a sixteen-by-twenty-one foot single-room house by the road, complete with a seven foot square basement. The basement could be reached through either a trap door in the house floor, or either one of two exterior doors, which seem to have been always locked. There was also a sort of tunnel, which may have been used to lever in a monstrous seven-foot slab of rock, which became the cellar floor—or maybe the tunnel had other uses too, especially in the hours between midnight and dawn.

The house would be the family dwelling, and would also do further duty as a sort of primitive country-store-cum-bed-and-breakfast, advertised by a crude sign that read "Grocry" until Kate turned the sign over and neatly spelled "Groceries" correctly. The Bender womenfolk arrived sometime in the winter of 1871, and their crude inn was soon open for business.

For a while Kate spent some time waiting tables at the restaurant in a hotel in newly minted Cherryvale. That there were then two hotels in that nearby town by December of 1873 is some indication of the increasing traffic on the Osage track. She apparently held the job only a few weeks, until the spirit moved—literally—and she heeded the call to visit the spirit world, and ultimately to embark on a budding career as a spiritualist and psychic healer.

So far, although the senior Benders won no popularity contests, at least Pa was known to spend some time reading his German Bible—you can't be all bad if you read the Good Book—and Kate and Young Joe attended Sunday school. But a little at a time the initial good, or at least neutral, impression of people in the area began to change.

For one thing, the much-admired Kate was accused of larceny of a sidesaddle left with her by a woman who used it to secure Kate's "healing" fee.

And a man—probably well in his cups—told a tale of seeing Kate and another woman dancing naked by firelight to strange music. In another instance, when a doctor interrupted a Bender healing session with his patient, he was disturbed by the anger he saw in Kate's face.

Right up there with the naked dancing in the theater of the bizarre was another woman's description of her last visit to the Bender homestead, of witnessing there the Bender men plunging knives into crude pictures of men drawn on the house walls. That memorably unpleasant evening ended when Kate confided that the spirits told her to kill her visitor, who fled into the night. Consistent with that tale is the story of someone who saw satanic images and figurines in the Bender shack.

And then there were the disappearances. During the terrible winter of 1872, two men turned up in the area with their throats cut and their skulls fractured. Later that year a man named John Boyle disappeared after he set out to buy some land; he was carrying almost $1,900 to finance his real estate transactions, a very great deal of money in that far-off year.

On and on those unsettling stories continued to circulate in the Cherryvale area of Labette County: rumors of travelers simply disappearing without trace. As early as the autumn of 1869 one Joe Sowers set out for Kansas and simply vanished. So did a man called Jones somewhat later. He later turned up, what was left of him, in a water hole, with a smashed skull and his throat cut all the way across.

One day a fop in a chinchilla coat stopped in at the Benders' place for a drink and was not seen again. Another traveler drove up in a fine new wagon pulled by two matched horses, and also vanished. The worst tragedy was a man called George Lonchar, who had lost his wife and was taking his little daughter to stay temporarily with her grandparents; both were simply . . . gone.

Even men of the cloth were not immune, like a priest scared away from the Benders' "Inn" after he saw Pa Bender with a hammer in his hand, whispering conspiratorially with Kate. And then there was William Pickering, a well-dressed traveler who wanted toast instead of cornbread; he also elected to sit on the side of the table away from the canvas wall that separated the eating area from the rest of the crude house, and he saw several greasy spots on the canvas about head level. Kate, however, insisted that he take the usual seat.

A bitter argument with the lovely Kate followed, and at last Pickering announced that if he couldn't eat on the clean side of the table he wouldn't eat there at all. At which Kate pulled a knife on him, and Pickering departed in some haste.

What finally broke the reign of terror was the disappearance of Dr. William York, from whom Lonchar had bought a team and wagon before he disappeared with his daughter. When Dr. York heard about the disappearance of Lonchar and his little girl, he rode down to aid in the search. When a half-starved team was found abandoned, he identified the famished horses as those he had sold to Lonchar.

And then the doctor was gone too, vanished like the others. There was evidence that he had stopped for the night at Bender's and he was known to have been carrying several hundred dollars and riding a fine-blooded horse. In light of what the neighbors later learned, his possessions and his interest in the Lonchar family were a certain death warrant.

Dr. York's disappearance summoned up Nemesis at last, in the person of Dr. York's brother, a very tough soldier, Colonel Alexander York. The colonel rode out to find out what happened to his brother. He brought along still another brother, Ed York, and the persistence of the two spelled the end of the Benders' comfortable life of murder and robbery. The brothers York dug so deeply that the Benders disappeared virtually overnight, telling nobody and leaving starving stock behind them. For the brothers had talked to as many residents as they could find, and had even hired local help to drag waterways and beat their way through thick brush. With a crew that one writer estimated at fifty helpers, the brothers covered a lot of ground, and didn't look like stopping any time soon.

They had interviewed the Benders, and had gone away both suspicious and unconvinced by what they had learned. The son had invented a fable about himself, a yarn about being ambushed and shot at; he even led the brothers to the alleged site of the shooting. The second act had been Kate's boasting about her prowess as a healer and seer. Neither sibling impressed the investigators in the slightest, and it was a given that the sourpuss elder Benders would have created a very bad impression.

No doubt the vexing investigation of the York brothers provided part of the impetus, but what probably told the Benders that the game was up was a mass meeting of local men, which resolved that all the residents ought to open their farms to a search. It was apparently unanimously approved, and so the handwriting was on the wall. If the Benders refused to open their land and building for inspection, they would immediately become the center of suspicion. If they did invite inspectors in, just a little investigation might reveal the horrors on their property.

And so the family elected to run for it, between, as it were, midnight and dawn.

The news brought neighbors out in force after the Benders vanished from their shack, and it was not long before a sharp set of eyes spotted a depression in the earth in one of the few small areas ever cultivated by the Benders. The searchers began to probe, found a soggy depression and very shortly uncovered the body of the colonel's brother, buried facedown in a shallow grave.

Everybody remembered the mysterious series of disappearances that had plagued this end of Labette County; now that one body had turned up and there were solid suspects, digging on a larger scale began immediately. Very soon large groups of citizens were turning over the earth near the Bender shanty, shoveling grimly in a stench of putrefaction as they uncovered victim after victim.

How the murders had been committed came slowly to light. When the crude Bender hostel was fitted out for company, a canvas curtain or tarpaulin was hung from the ceiling to separate the minuscule "restaurant" area from the family's tiny private space. The kitchen table sat in front of the canvas, and guests were ordinarily seated at the table with their backs to the canvas. Dinner was served by one of the Bender women, but food was not all some of the unfortunate guests got.

The story goes that while the guest was being entertained inside, some family member checked his wagon or horse, including his luggage or saddlebags. That gave the family some notion of the desirability of turning him into a corpse; there were risks, they knew. Sooner or later somebody might come looking for the traveler, and so the potential loot had to be worth the gamble.

Once the victim was comfortably seated at his meal, and his possessions inspected, the stage was set for the hulking Pa Bender: once the guest was occupied and off his guard, Pa simply stepped up with one of his three hammers, and caved in the diner's skull. Maybe he sometimes struck through the canvas—there were suspicious stains on it at about the right height—or he simply stepped around it and struck his victim.

Then the remains were quickly shoved through the trapdoor into the basement, where one or more family members cut the man's throat. The cellar floor was soaked with blood; the stench was overpowering. And if that were not enough, the searchers found scattered bullet holes, as if hammers and knives had not been enough for some of the tougher victims.

The digging turned up one horror after another. The bodies were largely naked, and at least one had been badly hacked up, as if in a fury of rage. If the sight of the corpses and the stench of putrefaction were not enough, what really turned the stomachs of the searchers was the little girl. Alone of all the victims, the little Lonchar girl had not been cut or battered, rather she had been, as the examining doctor grimly concluded, buried alive.

The temper of the crowd was also not improved by the sight of much of the Bender stock, which had simply been abandoned. The family had done nothing to even marginally protect the beasts, not even turn them loose to fend for themselves. The searchers were sickened by the sight of dead animals, and some still living that had long been deprived of food and even water.

Nobody is sure of the tally of the dead. There is pretty general agreement about the bodies actually found, eleven of them, plus an assortment of body parts which could not be reassembled into a whole. What happened to the missing pieces remains a mystery. There are any number of ugly stories about Kate; one of them has her bedding man after man, even sleeping with her cousin; and "whenever she had a baby they would just knock it in the head."

There are other guestimates of the number of the murdered, ranging from eight through eleven—there were certainly that many—on up to twenty and "pretty near forty."

And there may be some truth somewhere in the mass of mythology that has followed the killings. One story laments a young married couple, who stopped at the Benders and never left; the groom murdered, and the bride raped by both John and Pa before she too was killed.

It seems reasonable to suppose there were more victims than were ever found. The body parts account for some of them, but since murdering strangers was a way of life for the bloody Benders, there is a measurable chance that today's sophisticated electronic gear might reveal anomalies in the old Bender property that could lead to more graves.

Once it was obvious that the Benders had fled, several searches were launched. The governor of Kansas announced a reward of $500 a head, and another $1,000 was put up by Colonel York. There were also arrests and rumors of arrests of other people, none of which came to anything.

Journalists flocked to the scene, and visitors by the hundreds went away with some piece of the old homestead as a treasured souvenir. As the Thayer *Headlight* put it, "The whole of the house, excepting the heavy framing timbers . . . and even the few trees, have been carried away by the relic hunters."

The searches went on, and so did the stories. One tale declares that the Benders were run down "on the prairie," and killed on the spot, Kate being singled out to be burned alive, the traditional fate of a witch. Others said the searches found nothing, or that all four Benders were caught and hanged forthwith, without benefit of clergy.

One tale with the ring of truth relates that the Benders got away by train, their progress traced by recollections of railroad employees of the luggage, which included not only a white bundle but a "dog hide trunk," whatever that may be. One search led across the Oklahoma border to Vinita, where detectives got word of four Germans, the youngest of whom told a local man that the four wanted to go far west to an "outlaw colony."

The detectives seemed to know of this place, a dismal sort of hideout where a collection of fugitives lived like troglodytes in dugouts, a foul place where any lawmen who entered stood a very good chance of never coming out again. That lead petered out, but the search went on. The lawmen found traces of their quarry somewhere north of El Paso. There the searchers gave it up.

There are other variations on the tale, leading to the family's ultimate unhappiness with living in or near the "outlaw colony." This story had Kate leaving first, bugging out with a transient painter who later deserted her. The same tale has the old folks leaving too, until Pa deserted Ma, taking with him the remaining loot.

There are many more tales, one of them being that Colonel York stayed on the trail and killed both Kate and John. There is a particularly wild story told by a man named Ayers who said he discovered his new wife was Kate Bender. He told about the time his "coffee was drugged and I knew nothing more for fourteen days." A friend saved him after he was clouted on the head and dumped on the railroad tracks. The same story said two other men who saw Mrs. Ayers confirmed she was Kate Bender.

The story goes that Labette County wanted no part of an expensive and problematical prosecution.

Other tales abound, one of the best told by one Collins, of Rio Vista, California. A woman there, "found dead in a resort she conducted," had told him that she was the much sought-for Kate, but swore him to secrecy while she lived. Once she died, of course, there was no way to be sure of her identity.

There is much, much more to the supposition about the ultimate fate of the repulsive Benders, all of it entertaining, but far too convoluted to be included here. It has been ably explored by more than one writer, particularly Fern Morrow Wood, in *The Benders: Keepers of the Devil's Inn*.

"Devil's Inn" is an apt description. Whatever the family's subsequent fate, you have to suspect it involved a strong odor of brimstone.

CHAPTER FOUR

Machinegun Kate

Ma Barker

There is no more bizarre tale in the annals of crime than the story of the Barker gang. Part of it real, part of it modern myth, much of it overdramatization and downright invention by journalists writing for a public hungry for anything that could help it forget the dismal days of the Great Depression. All of it is ugly.

The so-called Barker gang was not the monolithic crime machine as it is sometimes portrayed. Individual members often ran alone or hooked up for a job with other professional criminals, like Alvin Karpis—lovingly known as "Creepy Karpis"—Ray Terrill, and the psychotic killer Larry DeVol. But the Barkers were also in part a family unit, which made them wonderful newspaper copy; best of all their guiding light was a woman—and not only a woman, but their mother. Anyhow, according to journalistic myth and J. Edgar Hoover, that is.

The tale grew and flourished that "Ma" Barker, as she was inevitably called, was the gang's planner, organizer, and evil genius, that she directed the family criminal operations, and in fact fought beside her boys. It's a fascinating idea, and has produced thousands of words of exciting copy. The tale will probably never die, but the truth seems to have been far more prosaic. Still, her fanciful reputation as gang leader and planner continues, in part due to the Barkers' arch-nemesis, the iconic FBI director J. Edgar Hoover.

Ma Barker began life as Arizona Donnie Clark, born in the Ozark Hills northwest of Springfield, Missouri, back in 1873. She was called

Arrie or Kate as a youngster, and while she was still in her teens, she married plodding George Barker and began to give birth to a series of hoodlums. The brothers—four of them—found a choice spot in criminal history as the Barker gang: Herman (called Slim), Freddy (Shorty), Arthur (Doc or Dock), and Lloyd (Red).

The kids got into trouble early and often, and father George shrugged off any responsibility: "You have to talk to Mother," he would say. "She handles the boys." Mother would then "handle the boys" by waxing vitriolic toward whomever complained about her little angels' misdeeds, sure that they were being persecuted. J. Edgar Hoover's comment that she was "a monument to the evils of parental indulgence" seems to have been right on the money.

None of her sons were very bright, and there are all sorts of stories about them, not least that they were all homosexual save Dock. The same has been said of sometime gang members Karpis and Volney Davis, and may or may not be true; the same may or may not be true of the tale that Fred and Karpis were lovers. There is a truly ugly tale told by sometime gang member Blackie Audett, that Karpis went out into the countryside to "find these poor, dumb farm girls . . . [Ma Barker] would abuse these poor girls terrible, and then Freddie and Karpis and that fag Volney Davis would kill the girls at Ma's order when old lady Barker was done playing with them . . . why there must be thirty or forty bodies . . . still at the bottom of a half dozen Minnesota lakes."

There's no question that Audett said it; whether it's all true or all hogwash or some of each, nobody will ever know for sure. For example, Volney Davis was lover to Edna "Rabbit" (or "Rabbits") Murray, which makes you wonder about Audett's appellation of "fag" for him, but anything was possible with this fragrant coterie.

So Ma may have preferred women—or not—depending on what source you read, even been a corrupter of young girls, but her enduring legacy is of criminal mastermind, planner, evil inspiration, leader of the pack. J. Edgar Hoover called her "the most vicious, dangerous and resourceful criminal brain of the last decade," which was saying quite a lot.

Now, lack of anything resembling a functional brain is, and was, a common criminal characteristic, and seems to run in families. The Barker

Ma Barker

boys were no exceptions, being both slow-witted and vicious, an almost certain recipe for disaster. They badly needed leadership, and the folk history of the Barker gang says that leadership came from Ma. If it really did, she either gave lousy advice and leadership, or the boys paid no attention to good counsel, if any, for the boys were a series of disasters.

Dock murdered a man in Oklahoma in 1922, and spent the next ten years in "Big Mac"—McAlester Prison, as tough a place as any this side of Alcatraz. Once out, he lost no time in returning to what he did best, brutalizing other people. He ran with several other very bad men, including his brother Fred and Creepy Karpis.

Bank robbery and murder were Dock's line of work, until he graduated to the big time. Along with brother Fred, Karpis, and other veteran criminals, he hit the top of the criminal world with the successful kidnappings of Edward Bremer and William Hamm. Both well-publicized crimes produced large paydays, which should have been enough to finance a quiet retirement for the whole family.

Hamm was the heir to the Hamm Brewery fortune, and Bremer's wealthy family was also financed by a brewery, among other things. The Hamm kidnapping was worth $100,000; the Bremer job twice that, both ransoms paid in cash. The bills were marked, of course, but there were places in the underworld where a canny hoodlum could swap the hot money for clean bills, paying a substantial percentage, of course.

All that money should have financed years of comfort, plus a little frivolity. But instead of retiring, Doc remained a working outlaw into 1935, when the newly christened "G-Men" hauled him off to face the rest of his life in prison, and not just any prison—this time it was the formidable Rock: Alcatraz. Nobody was ever known to escape; if you managed to get past the guard force and the walls, you still had to face the deadly tides of San Francisco Bay. Doc tried it in 1939, and predictably the guard force won.

Brother "Slim" ran with the so-called Barker-Inman-Terrill gang, robbing banks across the Midwest and murdering at least two police officers. At last, cornered by police and badly shot up, he committed suicide. At least he saved the taxpayers some money.

As will appear, Ma was present when the road also ended for son Fred, which left Lloyd William, who would be the last of the Barkers. He answered to either "Bill" or "Red," and was a veteran of service in World War I; he actually received an honorable discharge.

He was left out of much of his siblings' nefarious doings, having been laid by the heels after a 1921 mail robbery in Baxter Springs, Kansas. That got him twenty-five years in Leavenworth, where he remained until the autumn of 1938. Red went back to the Army and worked as a cook during World War II, gaining not only another honorable discharge but a Good Conduct Medal.

He took a job at a Denver bar and grill when he got out and lived on until the spring of 1949, when his wife became sufficiently irritated with him to blow him away with a shotgun. The lady was not operating on all eight cylinders, it appears, but Red was dead nevertheless.

Ma tried always to be close to her vicious offspring, and she is said to have resented any attention the boys paid to real women. She was always quick with her endless litany of poor excuses for their foul behavior, too, even as kids. In Ma's eyes somebody else was always to blame: society, the teacher, the police, whoever. As her long-suffering husband later complained, Ma would never correct her sons for anything, but only blame other people for her kids' misconduct. And it may have been his attempt to finally draw a line in the sand about the boys that finished their marriage; one story says that he insisted that Lloyd be punished for a criminal offense, arousing Ma's lasting indignation. George got the gate.

However she was later played in the movies, Ma was no femme fatale. Any photograph of dumpy, dowdy, very ordinary Ma suggests how unlikely a passionate extramarital liaison was, but in 1928 or thereabouts, she nevertheless traded off old dull husband George for a lover, one Arthur Dunlop.

Whether Ma simply got tired of George or became enamored of Dunlop is not recorded. There is evidence that George maybe had had enough of wild criminal children and a wife who refused to even try to rein them in or tolerate an attempt to do so by George or anybody else.

Dunlop was no matinee idol and he talked far too much, but he remained Ma's consort until he ended up in rural Wisconsin, naked as a jay bird and dead with a single bullet hole in his head. His abrupt departure came about either because Ma was tired of him or because her gentle offspring thought him a risk to go to the police, or at least talk so loudly that the law would come calling.

Ma's departure from this life was as colorful and improbable as the rest of her myth. She was holed up with son Fred when the FBI caught up with him hiding out on Lake Weir, near Ocklawaha, Florida, January 16, 1935. After much shooting—one source says the feds fired until they ran out of ammunition—the FBI closed in to find both Fred and Ma filled full of holes and very dead. The story goes that a Thompson submachinegun was found in Ma's hands—or near her—depending on which version you read. More newspaper space was devoted to a sinister radio that was turned on "all day" and the fact that both of the Barker's cars were equipped with radios, not a common thing back then.

The press had a field day. For example, the Jacksonville, Florida Times-Union predictably described the federal fire as "withering" and lavished no end of purple prose on the great "six-hour" gunfight, like this: "Machineguns were found beside the bodies of both victims. 'Machinegun Kate' and her son had no intention of being taken alive."

"Machinegun Kate?" That would fit with the myth of Ma as the leader of the pack, vicious to the end, but there's also a theory that J. Edgar Hoover, uneasy about killing a mother—even a Barker mother—stage-managed that incriminating scene, inventing the tale that Ma was found with the "Chicago piano" beside her. And Hoover produced that deathless twaddle about Ma being "the most vicious, dangerous and resourceful criminal brain of the last decade."

There were other, far different opinions. Asked about Ma's leadership and planning of the gang's criminal forays, veteran robber Harvey Bailey wrote, "That old woman couldn't plan breakfast," or something like that. "When we'd sit down to plan a bank job, she'd go in the other room and listen to Amos and Andy or hillbilly music on the radio."

And Alvin Karpis described the allegedly Machiavellian "Machinegun Kate" thus:

> [S]he wasn't a leader of criminals or even a criminal herself . . . an old-fashioned home-body from the Ozarks . . . superstitious, gullible, simple, cantankerous, and well, generally law-abiding. The most ridiculous story in the annals of crime is that Ma Barker was the mastermind behind the . . . gang. . . . [S]he knew we were criminals but her participation in our careers was limited to one function: when we traveled together, we moved as a mother and her sons. What could look more innocent?

And, like Bailey, Alvin was in a position to know.

"Machinegun Kate" Ma Barker certainly wasn't. But the whole era has produced reams of "historical" prose on the Barkers, and there has been much speculating about Ma's status and other details of the Weir Lake fight. Certainly Hoover produced a great deal of prose about that battle, all of it plainly calculated to inflate the role and reputation of the FBI, and not incidentally, his own. This in addition to being a neat apologia for the death of somebody's mother.

And as usual, the movies have had a field day with the Ma Barker story, also as usual with not a whole lot of attention to accuracy. One of the really enjoyable films was *Bloody Mama*, starring Shelley Winters, complete with submachinegun. If it makes it to television, and if you don't take it as serious history, *Bloody Mama* is well worth watching. You can, among other spectacles, watch not only Ma but all her sons get killed in one giant shootout. It doesn't resemble what really happened, but then, Hollywood never worried overmuch about historical accuracy.

Ma inspired a good deal of other Hollywood claptrap, such readily forgettable films as *Ma Barker's Killer Brood* and *Public Enemies*, plus mentions in television's *The Untouchables* and elsewhere. Her legend as criminal mastermind is far too solidly established now to be undone, at least in the public's mind.

So passed the Barker boys and their momma. Other gang members came to similarly unpleasant ends. Alvin Karpis—sometimes called Old Creepy—was in the thick of many of the Barker clan's lethal adventures. A long-time close observer of his fellow hoodlums, he rates a few sentences.

Karpis was Canadian by birth, but he fit right in with all-American hoodlums like the Barkers and the punks who ran with them. His best buddy and running mate was Fred Barker, with whom he shared both some jail time and a budding career robbing banks. By the end of 1931 they were wanted for several robberies and the murder of at least two law officers.

For a while Karpis and Fred had lived with Ma at White Bear Lake in Minnesota. Nobody knew them there, and they could busy themselves with housebreaking and other minor crimes. Karpis hungered for more. And so, early in 1932, along with Fred, the murderous sadist Larry DeVol, and two other men, he drove south to Concordia, Kansas, to hit a bank. What happened after that is one of the classic stories of Depression-era crime.

The planning was elaborate, involving carefully casing the bank, holding a get-away rehearsal, and stashing gasoline cans at appropriate spots along the line of retreat. They even left coffee and sandwiches at one of their gas dumps; you had to feed the inner man, after all. They paid great attention to detail, right down to a supply of corks to plug any gas-tank holes police bullets might make, and overalls—the better to blend in with the bucolic nature of the town.

The robbery went like clockwork, and the gang quickly cleaned out the tellers' cash drawers. Customers and staff were herded into a back room and the only bank employee who knew the combination to the vault was ordered to open it. Then came the snag, a great moment in the history of American crime. "No," quoth the bank man simply, "no," and no amount of death threats to him or his coworkers could change his mind.

"I ain't openin' no vault for anybody," he said, and that was that; no amount of tough talk could change his position. Fred waved his gun around and DeVol threatened to burn out the bank man's eyes, but the answer remained simply, "no."

So some of the hardest of the professional criminals ended up retreating without their momentous payday, for which they had so carefully plotted. They got more than $20,000 from the cash drawers, but that sure wasn't the bonanza they had planned on, and the damage to their egos must have been substantial.

Curses! Foiled again!

Other small bank robberies followed, but the end of the rainbow remained elusive. And so, in December 1932, the gang tried on the Third Northwestern National Bank of Minneapolis. This time it would be Doc and Fred Barker and an assortment of other punks, including one with the curious nickname of "Lapland Willie." They were armed with no fewer than four submachineguns—anybody could buy a Thompson in those less-regulated days, even by mail order.

Karpis was probably along too, although he later said he wasn't; he had to go assist Ma Barker, he said, because she had told him she had a heart attack. Nobody wants to admit to being part of murder, even Karpis. For that is what happened.

In the first place, the building lacked cover and concealment; it was, as Karpis put it, "like working in a greenhouse." Worse, somebody fired the silent alarm and a pair of officers drove up in front of the bank.

DeVol and another punk sprayed the police car with tommy gun fire and both officers went down, one dying, the other mortally wounded. They never had a chance, and the fat was now well into the fire. To compound the problem, as the gang switched cars during the getaway, a stranger drove slowly by.

Fred assumed he was writing down their license number. The man wasn't. He was a good Samaritan who had merely slowed down to see if these people needed help. What he got was a fatal bullet from Fred's pistol. The gang hid out in Reno for a time, and then it was back to the old grind again, a series of holdups and the gang's piece de resistance, the Hamm and Bremer kidnappings.

Then and afterward, Karpis assiduously reinforced his own myth. He was, he said, a sort of latter-day Robin Hood, taking from the rich and giving to the poor, helping all the poor people forced off their ancestral land by those heartless banks. That was arrant nonsense, of course, but in those hard times it appealed to a lot of ordinary folks.

Karpis stayed free for another sixteen months or so after the Lake Weir fight, until the FBI caught up with him in New Orleans in May of 1936. He was taken without a fight, allegedly personally captured by J. Edgar Hoover, although another version of the apprehension tells that only after other agents safely secured Karpis did Hoover appear to formally arrest him.

Hoover certainly made much capital of the event, however it really went down. He and the Bureau got the glory, and Karpis got the time. He went off to join his old comrade Doc Barker, who had already gone to Alcatraz and would die in his abortive escape attempt in 1939. Karpis would spend the next thirty-some years in the federal prison system, most of it on the Rock.

While in Alcatraz he took pity on a young convict who'd spent a lifetime in various institutions; and so Karpis decided to "do something for him" and began to teach the youngster to play the guitar. Karpis later said of his young charge, "There was something unmistakably unusual about [him] . . . a runt of sorts, but found his place as an experienced manipulator of others. I did feel manipulated, and under circumstances where it hadn't been necessary." Small wonder. The punk he had befriended was Charles Manson, as weird and murderous a psychopath as ever walked, who became the mystic guru of a band of murderous misfits.

If Ma Barker was at all the gang's inspirational leader, she had much to answer for. None of it was good.

CHAPTER FIVE

Rank Amateur

Pearl Hart

One of the more appealing members of the Bad Girls' club was a little waif called Pearl Hart. Pearl was a diminutive lady, as her multitude of photographs testify. Whether she had her picture taken as a modestly dressed female, or as a convict, or as a tough outlaw in men's clothing, she remained the Girl Next Door.

Like so many of the fair sex in the outlaw world, her deeds and her personality are shrouded to this day in a swirling mist of mythology. She was grandiloquently called the Bandit Queen in some accounts, more elegantly the Lady Bandit in others. The truth was far more prosaic. In fact, Pearl was a mine-camp cook, or maybe a prostitute, or maybe a singer, depending on which story you read, or maybe all of these, seriatim or all at once.

She was Canadian by birth, said to have come from a respectable middle-class family, and even to have attended "finishing school." She ran off with a sometime gambler and barkeep, a perennial ne'er-do-well named Frederick Hart. He was worthless by all accounts, brutal, lazy, and unpleasant, and that was on his good days. Pearl succumbed to such charm as Hart had when she was a susceptible sixteen, and life got progressively tougher from there.

In 1893, Pearl and Hart went to the Columbian Exposition in Chicago, where Pearl attended Wild West shows and, according to some accounts, fell head over heels in love with the images of the Wild West. Hart worked as a side-show barker while they were in Chicago, and Pearl did "odd jobs," not further specified.

Pearl Hart

Pearl moved abruptly to Colorado, where she produced a son, which she took to her parents' home. Then it was back to the West once more, this time to Phoenix, where she worked as a cook and laundress. Hart showed up out of the blue in 1895, and Pearl unadvisedly took him back, a pointless evolution that she would go through more than once.

Pearl had two children by Hart—well, one was his for sure, but maybe the other was by somebody called Dan something-or-other. That child she also left with her patient parents in Canada. In the fullness of time she again got heartily sick of Hart's sloth and brutality, left him repeatedly, and took him back almost as often.

At last even Pearl had had enough, and returned to Arizona, the land of her dreams. The mythology gets thick here. Some tales of Pearl cast her as an early-day feminist, inspired by watching Annie Oakley at the Chicago Columbian Exposition in 1883 and listening to suffragette speeches there.

As the final straw, in 1898 the noxious Hart exploded once too often and beat Pearl badly. He wasn't going to have any more of this marriage stuff, he said, and departed to join the Rough Riders and sample the war in Cuba. Pearl was on her own again, drifting from one mining camp to the next as a cook. Or, as another story tells, Pearl turned her hand to whatever came along, cooking, performing, turning tricks, whatever, until she heard that her mother was grievously ill and in need of money. It was then she turned to crime, it is said, purely to raise money for mama, or at least that was what Pearl told a jury later on.

By now Pearl was deeply depressed, and tried suicide; friends intervened and she survived. She got work as a camp cook at Mammoth, living in a tent, her health declining. It was here that she took up with feckless Joe Boot, variously described as a miner, a cowboy, or a musician. Joe wanted to go to Globe. She went with him, and went to work as a cook in a miner's boarding house; that is, she did until a big mine shut down and she was again unemployed.

Reenter the egregious, omnipresent Hart. This time Pearl refused to support this lazy slob, and he left, never, fortunately, to be seen again. And about this time somebody wrote her that her mother was seriously ill and if she wanted to see mom alive she must come quickly. But Pearl had no money for train fare back to Canada. What to do?

Reenter Joe Boot, who told her he had a fine mining claim: Let's go there, he said, and we'll dig out a bunch of pay dirt and live high on the hog. They did, and Pearl swung a pick and shovel just as he did, but the results were disappointing: Lots of dirt, no pay.

Some sources say Pearl was the moving force in inspiring Joe to forsake the paths of righteousness for the fast lane. Legend says that at first they played a version of the age-old badger game. The two rolled passersby interested in a roll in the hay with Pearl, still something of a looker by all accounts. Once in her room, however, enter Joe, who whopped the avid stranger on the dome and took his money. That ploy either proved to be too dangerous, or it didn't pay enough.

The story of the badger game may also have been the basis for another tale that has them running a brothel. Whether Pearl was the whole staff, or managed the enterprise or both, that enterprise also proved to be a nonstarter.

When both the claim and the purveyance of carnal delights turned out to be a bust, Joe proposed they rob the Globe stage, or maybe Pearl was the criminal mastermind. She was reluctant by some accounts, but finally decided it was her ticket to Canada. They posted themselves near a curve where they knew the stage would have to slow down. When the stage got close, they rode down the road, and when they met the stage, hauled out their handguns. It all worked as they had planned, and Pearl ordered the passengers out into the road.

She found a couple of pistols stashed down in the passengers' seats and took those, a casual act that would generate a vast amount of trouble for Pearl later on. Then the passengers were forced to pungle up. Most of them didn't have much money, but one passenger was carrying almost $400, which would buy a lot of railroad tickets. There is a story that Pearl, all heart, gave each of the victims back a buck to eat on. There was no violence, and the tyro robbers rode off toward Benson, where they intended to catch a train and disappear.

So far, so good, but now their amateur status became obvious. They clearly had not planned their escape; they immediately made a tyro mistake, which would prove terribly costly. They camped on the east bank of the Gila River, but instead of moving on quickly, they inexplicably stayed a full twenty-four hours, not riding on until the next night. The next camping spot was close to a lot of road traffic, so they sought out a cave, shooting a wild boar that was there first.

Next night they rode on; Joe went into the town of Mammoth to get some supplies, and they kept moving. Rain was pouring down, their horses were bone weary, and so they camped for another full day, moving on again that night. According to one account, by now they were hopelessly lost, and abruptly found themselves back on the stage road only a little way from the site of the holdup.

That discovery had to have been a considerable shock, but instead of moving on, however weary the two were, about five o'clock the next morning they made camp again and drifted off to sleep. Some three hours later they were unpleasantly awakened to be greeted by the baleful stare of the bores of a couple of rifles. The owners turned out to be members of a sheriff's posse, and Joe and Pearl were out of the crime business.

Joe took up residence in the jail at Florence, county seat of Pima County, where the holdup actually took place. Pearl tried suicide—again—but guards stopped her, and she was moved to Tucson, where there were better accommodations for women. Pearl wasn't through. After supper one night she used a knife from the jail silverware to dig out bricks from the jail wall. She managed to dig a hole in her cell wall large enough to slither through, and vanished into the night.

Caught with a male companion (not the useless Joe Boot) by lawman extraordinaire George Scarborough, Pearl was "in a state of undress." She told Scarborough she couldn't possibly go with him, all her clothing being in the Chinese laundry. Scarborough was not sympathetic. "So dress in your boyfriend's clothing," he said, and back she went to jail. She was, said Scarborough, one of the most foul-mouthed people he had ever heard.

At trial, Pearl turned on the tears for the jurors. "I only got involved because I had to get home to mama," she said, "and I had no money. I would never have done this otherwise, only out of devotion to my mother." And it worked. Acquitted in spite of the evidence, Pearl rejoiced. The judge did not. Quickly re-arrested, Pearl was tried for larceny of one of the pistols she had purloined during the holdup. This time a new jury saw the evidence in a different light and convicted her. The sentence was five years—not excessive, in view of the thirty-five the court had already laid on Joe.

After serving something like half her sentence, Pearl was pardoned. One lurid legend tells that she was pregnant when she got out, or said she was. That made the situation somewhat delicate, or so the story goes, since the only men who had been alone with her in her cell were a clergyman and the Territorial Governor. Well, maybe.

What is certain is that she became quite a celebrity while in jail, the center of attention of various writers, who cranked out fanciful stories and had her photographed carrying various firearms, presumably unloaded. Since the jailers had access to her too, the story about impregnation by state officials is a little thin . . . but it's too good a tale to leave out.

What happened to Pearl after that is uncertain. There is a tale that she went back north, intending to capitalize on her notoriety as the famous lady bandit. Or maybe she was to sing, or act in a play about her written by her sister. She was arrested as part of a ring of pickpockets, and again for buying some canned goods that had been stolen by somebody else.

Whatever she did, it doesn't seem to have been a smashing success, and she returned to Arizona. It may have been during this period that she developed an addiction to laudanum, not uncommon in that day.

What happened to Pearl in later days makes a nice warm, fuzzy ending to the tale of a very tough life. She married a rancher named Bywater, and lived the rest of her long life peacefully in Dripping Springs. Far from bank-robbing, she ended her days "gardening and writing in a diary." A writer who saw her said of her, "She was shy, retiring, and talked to nobody. At that stage of her life, I believe she wanted to disappear and did. She's lived a heckuva life and deserved a little peace."

Fast forward about twenty-five years for what may just be the best part of Pearl's legend. The story goes that an "elderly lady" walked into the Pima County Jail and asked to look the jail over. When asked why, she said, "Well, I'm Pearl Hart and spent some time here about twenty-five years ago and I would like to see my old cell." She was accommodated by the jail staff, thanked them, and walked away into history.

Pearl remained unrepentant, it is said, telling and retelling the tale of her undistinguished criminal career. Would she do it again? You bet, said Pearl. No doubt she would have enjoyed a latter-day fable that had her planning a robbery with none other than Jesse James, helping Jesse escape the law, and riding off into the sunset with him to her "hideout."

Never mind that Jesse had been dead since 1882, in which year Pearl would have been about eleven. A girl can dream, can't she?

CHAPTER SIX

The Rabbit

Edna Murray

She was born back in 1898, up in Marion, Kansas, and was christened Martha Edward Stanley. Very early in life she moved with her father to Oklahoma and went to work as a waitress at the grandly named Imperial Café in Sapulpa. She was an attractive youngster, and no shrinking violet where the men were concerned either; before she turned twenty she had been married twice, to men named Paden and Price. Both unions had gone to pieces in fairly short order, leaving her with a son, called Preston, and an appetite for excitement and the high life.

Still a very nubile lass with an eye for the boys, she next met and fell deeply in love with Volney Davis. Now Davis was not your ordinary country boy; he was a taste of the big time, a professional robber successful at his trade, and on the run from the police. Volney was an alum of Tulsa's Central Park gang, that famous training school for punks that produced, among other undesirables, Ma Barker's four poisonous offspring. He was by definition a career tough guy.

Maybe so, but even when Edna found out that her new flame was not only a career criminal but on the lam, she didn't seem to care at all. The story goes that only after she had fallen deeply in love did she learn who he really was. By that time it no longer mattered, if it ever had. She fell right into step with her paramour, but the delight of her new man didn't last for long. The law caught up with Volney in 1918 and put him away for life.

Edna then moved in with her sister Doris O'Connor—aka Vinta Stanley—who was living with another professional criminal named

Emory Connell. Emory had a sort of partner in crime, a jewel thief named Diamond Joe Sullivan. Edna married him as well, a marriage that lasted only briefly, until Diamond Joe was convicted of murder and duly executed.

Edna wasn't having a whole lot of luck, but she kept on trying.

After Diamond Joe shuffled off this mortal coil, Edna found herself another man, Jack Murray. Jack was still another thug, and this time Edna obviously decided that her new husband's profession was a promising career for her too, or maybe she decided that if you can't beat 'em, join 'em. Anyhow, the pair went off robbing together, hitting a series of banks.

And this was when—in the autumn of 1925—Edna acquired her deathless nickname. The man she kissed was named Southward, the kiss a small flippant gesture after she and Murray had robbed the man, a gesture that won her a measure of newspaper fame as the "kissing bandit."

It also got her twenty-five years in the Missouri State Penitentiary for Women, a stretch that she discontinued in May of 1927 by escaping. She stayed free for over four years until she was picked up in Chicago in early November of 1931. She broke out for just one day two months later, and a year after that sawed through some bars and was gone again.

It was this series of escapes that won the slippery lady her title of "The Rabbit," or "Rabbits," an accolade given for her remarkable ability to outwit her keepers. It was a title of some respect in the dark world of the criminal fraternity, and probably regarded in the same light by the law, albeit somewhat grudgingly. This writer could find no parallel record of escapes by a woman, particularly from a penitentiary, normally much more secure than a county jail or town lockup.

And the lady was just beginning.

Reenter Volney Davis, who had made his own unauthorized departure from prison in 1932. He and Edna, based in Aurora, Illinois, started their own crime wave, helped out by Edna's son, Preston, and soon made contact with the Barker gang (or Barker-Karpis gang). They fit right in, especially since Edna's sister Doris was now playing house with gang member Jess Doyle.

Edna and Volney were running with the big dogs now. Three of the leading lights of crime even showed up on their doorstep seeking shelter from the law. One was none other than John Dillinger, and with him were Homer Van Meter and Red Hamilton. Hamilton had been very badly shot up and needed medical treatment badly.

But there would be no doctor, for the underworld medical association wanted no part of Hamilton. Even Joseph P. Moran—called "Doc" of course—long-time underground physician to the underworld who had treated Hamilton before, refused to help. The suffering Hamilton lingered for agonizing days with spinal wounds and gangrene until he passed to his reward, whatever that would be. He got a sort of funeral—to which "The Rabbit" and Volney went—and an unmarked grave.

Doc Moran is worth a brief mention in passing. He had been an honor student at Tufts Medical School, but had a continuing—and losing—problem with ol' devil booze. He'd done time up at Joliet Prison for an abortion gone wrong, and while in prison hooked up with the bank-robbing fraternity. On his release he went back to practicing medicine through the front door and performing abortions and repairing shot-up hoodlums through the rear. This happy arrangement continued until he became so sodden that he was at last regarded as unreliable. He ended up quite dead as a result—of gang-related causes.

The year after the world was rid of Hamilton, 1935, there broke indictments of a number of the Barker-Karpis outlaws for conspiracy in the spectacular $200,000 kidnapping of Minnesota banker Edward Bremer. Edna was one of those indicted, and fled, this time with Jess Doyle, but not far or fast enough. She was caught in Pittsburg, Kansas, and sent off to jail to await trial—or to be returned to Missouri to finish her prison sentence. Kansas claimed her first.

It was not a happy time for Edna and her family. Not only was she back in jail, but her brother Harry was charged with aiding and abetting her. Worst of all, her son Preston was tried and convicted of the murder of a watchman down in Kansas. He got a life sentence. As for the Rabbit herself, she won a surprising acquittal in her conspiracy trial, but that didn't stop Missouri from dragging her back to finish her long-interrupted sentence for robbery, now with an additional two years tacked on for her escapes.

She would serve only another five years, thanks in part to her cooperation with the government, testifying against several sometime

Barker-Karpis gang members and various corrupt public servants. She also made the most of a good thing, marketing in print memoirs of her heady years of running with the gangster pack. "I was a Karpis-Barker Gang Moll" is a good example; not great literature, but surely appetizing food for the insatiable curiosity of the public for anything exciting.

Edna the Rabbit had enough of life in the fast lane, and withdrew to relative seclusion after she was placed on probation just five days before Christmas in 1940.

She died in San Francisco in 1966.

CHAPTER SEVEN

The Ghosts of Indian Territory

The Dalton Ladies

Except perhaps for the James-Younger brothers and Billy the Kid, no outlaw or outlaw aggregation has been written about more than the Dalton gang. Bob, Grat, Bill, and Emmett Dalton have achieved iconic proportions in the folklore of the American West. Much of it is true, some of it is pure claptrap, and a great deal of it is invention, but all of it is interesting.

But what of the women? There don't seem to be any blood relatives who played much part in the Dalton's outlaw ways and days, unless you count Mother Dalton, the long-suffering Adeline, a good woman who tried her best to raise a flock of kids with very little help. She did a good job of it with most of her brood of fifteen: the four outlaw boys, however, caused her nothing but sorrow.

There were indeed women who ran with the Dalton boys: those we're sure of, and a bunch more maybes. And although these women didn't gallop about waving six-guns—with one exception—they were a colorful, memorable bunch. The stars of the show were two:

Florence Quick, alias (probably) Flora Mundis, alias (maybe) Tom King. Or maybe the lady was called, or also called, Eugenia Moore. Bob met the fascinating Eugenia Moore out in New Mexico, in a very bad place called Silver City, a raw new town that writer Harold Preece aptly described as "Babylon-on-a-Pithead, a place of florid squalor, with money heaping the varnished keno tables and burro dung littering the bawdy streets."

It seems Eugenia was a school teacher in her early twenties, and, as Emmett Dalton put it, "pure of mind . . . unusually intelligent and

47

Bob Dalton and Eugenia Moore, Vinita, Indian Territory, 1889

courageous." She was also, Emmett said, "a fair telegrapher" and, of course a child of a "fine old Missouri family." Fine family or not, pure mind or not, according to Emmett's golden prose, Eugenia became both mistress and spy for Bob: "Riding up and down on the railroad from Parsons, Kansas, to Denison, Texas, she was constantly on the alert for bits of information which might prove of value to us She being a telegraph operator, she frequently overheard messages in the depots telling of money shipments." Unlikely, even though Emmett said it, and he should know—but then, Emmett said a lot of things.

By today's freeways, Parsons to Denison is some 280 miles, roughly five hours' continuous travel. Now consider the likelihood of an attractive young woman riding perpetually up and down this route on the railroad, cozying up to freight agents, eavesdropping on telegraphs, and then riding as much as two hundred miles to alert her lover, part of it probably on horseback, still leaving Bob with time to dash off and rob the railroad. Setting up one raid, says one writer, required her to sleep with a railroad messenger to get her crucial information.

Like much of Emmett's creative writing, the notion of peripatetic travel strains credulity beyond the breaking-point. It also leaves a lot more questions unanswered, like how this virginal schoolteacher abruptly morphed into the greatest horse thief of the decade.

And here the confusion sets in, for Eugenia is said to be in fact the notorious female horse thief Flo Quick, who also went by the handle of Tom King. Tom/Flo was the real thing, in spades, whether she was also Eugenia or not, and indeed whether Eugenia existed at all.

One of the sources says they are one and the same and maybe also Daisy Bryant too. Daisy is said to be the sometime mistress of outlaw Blackface Charlie Bryant—or perhaps she was his sister. Another writer tells of Eugenia's sideline: seducing solid citizens and then blackmailing them. Once she conceived a passion for Bob, she eavesdropped on the telegraph and rode about the countryside, "a full-blown beauty," "setting up robberies" for the gang. One source has her stealing five horses for the gang's use in the raid on Coffeyville.

Emmett also gives her credit for the raid at Lelaetta, out in California, appearing "resplendent in Spanish chaps and a brand-new sombrero."

That tale also depends on Emmett's accuracy: Consider that he also said his take in that raid amounted to some $9,400 in silver, which would weigh a nearly a ton. This weight he is supposed to have carried in a sack slung across his saddle.

At least the gang didn't forget their ladies, or so 'tis said. After their holdup at Red Rock they carried off "feminine finery meant for Bob's mistress, Flo Quick; Emmett's flame, Julia Johnson; and Bitter Creek's little inamorata, Rose Dunn." The same account records that the gang got away with "three or four boxes of silk stockings."

Note that Bob's great passion is called Flo Quick in this tale, instead of Eugenia Moore, which simply adds to the confusion over who was who in the Daltons' fabulous harem.

Now Tom King was a world-class horse thief, a real and remarkable outlaw woman whom Glen Shirley called "the most elusive horse thief operating in Oklahoma during the period" (the 1890s), which is quite an accolade, considering the very talented male competition the lady had. If she and Flo were the same woman, she would have been the ideal mate for Bob Dalton.

Flo in any case turned a lot of heads. Consider this paean from a Wichita Daily Eagle reporter: "If she was a man she would be a type of cavalier. She is an elegant rider, very daring. She has a fine suit of hair as black as a raven's wing and eyes like sloes that would tempt a Knight of St. John. . . . [Her] figure is faultless."

Caramba! What a woman!

Even allowing for a bit of hyperbole in the reporter's description of the lady, Flo was quite a looker. She was not above using those looks, as when she was tired of being in jail, which was regularly. On at least one recorded occasion she slyly used her ravens-wing hair and sloe-like eyes not only to leave the jail without permission, but to take with her the jailer, who was obviously not a Knight of St. John. Her abrupt departure was, a local newspaper dryly noted, "an elopement and not an escape."

Another paper said about the same thing: "It seems there is no jail that can hold her. . . . She is very cunning and clever. The . . . officers generally get her, but getting her does not seem to be of much use in curing the mania with which she is afflicted. She finds the same delight in horse stealing as other women would in reading novels or playing croquet. It is her ambition to be the most famous horse thief of her generation, and she had already taken more of them than any man in history."

One source also credits her with jumping bail at least once, and once ending her confinement by an early release because she was pregnant. Maybe it was Christian kindness[,] . . . maybe it was because nobody wanted to sit inside the jail with Flo to help her deliver.

Flo was plainspoken about her carnal agility. Once, on her way to jail in the custody of veteran Deputy Marshals Heck Thomas and Chris Madsen, she asked the name of the jailer at the lockup to which she was bound. And when Madsen asked in his thick Danish accent, "Vy do you vant to know?" Flo told him the truth: "Every jailer in Oklahoma has his price: If I know which one this is, I'll know his."

Madsen—also known to exaggerate from time to time—said later that she was "a heavy drinker and a dope fiend. It was the dope that killed her. . . . She caused me more trouble than all the other women I ever had anything to do with." An especially cherished memory was the day he took her to Oklahoma City to stand trial. The wagon trip lasted all one long afternoon, time that Flo used inventively: "She cursed and swore at me and called me all the vile names in existence . . . didn't stop more than ten minutes all the way. When we got there she was so hoarse she couldn't talk."

Flo was the epitome of a bandit's dream: attractive, smart, and of course courageous. She was the one, according to legend, who brought Bob and the gang up-to-date knowledge of good prospects for robbery and vital information on the law's traps and snares. This multi-talented lady had the same talents accorded the mysterious Eugenia Moore, for she was also an accomplished telegraphist, who could visit a telegraph office, sweet talk with the duty telegrapher, and listen to the clatter of the key, obtaining vital information on the shipment of bullion and the like. Or so the story goes.

When the gang was at the peak of their notoriety, Flo is supposed to have created a classic diversion to delay pursuit. The legend tells that she enticed a yokel into her bedroom and got him arrested, telling the law that he was Bob Dalton. Her dupe remained in jail as the law rejoiced, and the gang got clear—that is, until Deputy Marshal Chris Madsen took one look at the prisoner and told the officers they had the wrong man.

If this story is true—and even if it isn't—Flo was a busy and ingenious girl. In addition to giving Bob all manner of aid and comfort, Flo spent some time sharing hearth and home with a Guthrie butcher called Mundy and stole the odd horse or two on the side. One site of her occasional passionate trysts with Bob, their "love nest in Greer County," was found by pursuing lawmen. The birds had flown, however, taking along "Flo's wardrobe, including plenty of silky Montgomery Ward negligees." Wow!

Flo produced a massive amount of folklore, all about a passionate and continuing affair with Bob and his profound depression over her illness and death. Emmett wrote at length of Bob and Flo (take another grain of salt here), and declaimed in shared agony the depression that attacked Bob when it appeared Flo was entering the Valley of the Shadow.

Bob was plunged into black depression, as Flo sickened and declined. Emmett put it in almost poetic terms: "Autumn leaves were already falling in her dark eyes while yet summer tossed green and vital outside."

Bob finally received a letter from lawman Ben Canty, telling him that the light of his life was dead. "Boys," said the heartbroken gang leader, "boys, I don't care what happens to me now." Or, alternatively, flinging Canty's letter into the fire, Bob cried, "Now I will make them understand that 'Hell on earth' is a reality!"—whoever "them" might be.

Much of the best folklore about Flo turns on a photo taken with Bob in Vinita, Oklahoma. He is seated; she is standing with one hand on his shoulder. Various theories identify her as Flo Quick alias Tom King, or maybe Eugenia Moore or even Daisy Bryant, who may have been either sister or wife to outlaw Blackface Charlie Bryant. Or not. There is even a suggestion that maybe the lady is Julia Johnson's sister Lucy.

To complicate matters still further, there is a chance that Eugenia Moore—probably a real person and scout or information bringer for the Dalton gang, may have also been Flo Quick. Various writers have added to the mix, speculating about the real identity of Bob's alleged beloved; there are votes for Daisy Bryant and votes for Tom King.

And the pre-Coffeyville agony doesn't stop with Bob.

According to bandit folklore, Emmett had to leave his own grand passion behind as he followed Bob and Grat north toward Coffeyville and disaster. If you accept his own account of his departure, he had nearly as heartrending a farewell as his brother.

Positively wallowing in sentimentality, he told of his heartwrenching goodbye to his treasured Julia Johnson. He sat in the Johnson home, he says, listening to his beloved play the "big organ . . . melodies suffused with sadness, carrying some indefinable lament or reproach as if to remind one constantly of life's swift passing."

He sure was going into harm's way, to the very place where life could—and very nearly did—swiftly pass. Emmett, full of holes and clinging hard to life after the gang's debacle at Coffeyville, would have to wait a long time to culminate his passion for Julia.

Once Emmett breathed free air again, he managed to stay out of jail. He then married Julia Johnson, described in several accounts as his "childhood sweetheart," who, legend says, faithfully waited for him to complete his sentence. They tied the knot in Bartlesville, Oklahoma, on September 1, 1908. Emmett wrote afterward that Julia was his "inspiration" while he did time, and that she had patiently waited for him for fifteen years.

Emmett and Julia were married, all right, but it is far from certain that they were sweet on one another as kids. Julia figures prominently in Emmett's second book, *When the Daltons Rode (1931)*, but does not appear in *Beyond the Law (2009)*, his first book. And Julia was surely not the virginal, faithful childhood love Emmett's book made her out to be. By the time they were wed, Julia could call herself Julia Johnson Gilstrap Lewis, for she had a colorful history.

In *When the Daltons Rode*, Emmett told how he fell for Julia in the spring of 1887, a pretty story about how he rode his pony past a country church and heard organ music of the sort the angels must play. Investigating, he discovered Julia, sweet sixteen, seated at the organ making the world a brighter place. It's a fine story, but you have to find a way to ignore the evidence of Julia's granddaughter that Julia couldn't play a lick on any instrument.

There's a lot more about Julia in Emmett's second book, all kinds of romantic tales about her riding through the night to warn Emmett about an approaching party of lawmen. That makes for exciting reading, but it's hard to square with Emmett's later assertions that Julia knew nothing of his dastardly occupation until he was shot up at Coffeyville.

And then there's the story of "Their Last Meeting," which Emmett places very shortly before the Coffeyville raid. How he left her side at the Johnson home, near Vinita, and got to Tulsa in time to ride north, is unexplained. What is even harder to explain is how Emmett could visit Julia at her parents' home when both her mother and father had been dead for over a year. Love will find a way, I guess.

Later on, Emmett's step-granddaughter said flatly that Emmett and Julia were never sweethearts at the time of the raid. Instead, they met after Emmett was released from prison. Julia would never, the granddaughter said, have married somebody else had she been "so sweet on Emmett."

Anyhow, Julia had been married at least twice before, the first time to one Bob Gilstrap, said to be a half-blood Cherokee. That was in 1887, and two years later, on Christmas Eve, Gilstrap got himself killed in a shootout with a man called Leno. After Gilstrap lost his fight with Leno, Julia was alone, with her daughter Jennie Gilstrap, until the fall of 1902.

In that year, instead of waiting patiently for Emmett to finish his term, she married one Earnest Lewis. Julia doesn't seem to have had much judgment in men. Earnest turned out to be that same "Killer" Lewis who is supposed to have ridden with the storied lady bandit Tom King.

In one version Lewis died of the bullets of a lawdog with the engaging handle of Pussyfoot Johnson. In another, Lewis opened up on one peace officer without warning, killing him. A second officer, one Keeler, turned out to be tougher and faster than Lewis was. In any case, the Killer was history, and Julia was available again.

Julia may even have been married—or been semi-permanently attached—a third time before she wed Emmett. There is a persistent story that she wed an Indian named Whiteturkey somewhere along the way. A pioneer neighbor of Julia's, north of Tulsa, indeed refers to her as "Julia Gilstrap-Whiteturkey, who later married Earnest Lewis and is now Mrs. Emmett Dalton."

Julia was apparently a lady of some spirit—"feisty," folks would have called her in those days. There is a story that she took umbrage over a newspaper story about Lewis, written after his death. Where other widows might have succumbed to the vapors or written a peevish letter to the paper, Julia was moved to pursue the editor through the streets with a horsewhip. A feisty lady, indeed.

After Emmett got out of the pen and he and Julia married, they lived for a time in Bartlesville, Oklahoma. One writer says Emmett later lived in Tulsa for a while, where he was a "special officer" appointed to "handle the hardest of the hardcases." The couple moved to California about 1918.

For a time, Emmett was part of the burgeoning movie industry. He and former Coffeyville photographer John Tackett produced a potboiler about the outlaw days called, predictably, *Beyond the Law*. Emmett even starred in the film, which turned out to be a nonstarter. After that, Emmett dabbled in the construction business, apparently with more success.

Emmett visited Coffeyville in 1931, long after the citizens' bitter animosity had died away to a dull ache. Julia came with him, and Emmett at last had a headstone carved and set up for Bob, Grat, and poor old friendless Powers, in place of the pipe to which they had tethered their horses all those years before. The pipe, incidentally, was left in place at the head of the graves. It is still there.

Emmett was sixty when he came to visit, and mellow with the years. He spent some time with a *Kansas City Star* reporter, walking over the scene of the fight. The result was some truly fulsome prose, the most modest of which was a purported quote from outlaw Henry Starr, who called Emmett "the nerviest, gamest, loyalest long rider of the whole wild bunch." Whatever. A dubious memorial, considering that Starr had spent much of his own life down with wounds or in jail, and would get himself permanently dead in a botched Oklahoma robbery.

The story of Emmett's farewell introduced Julia with a gooey quote from Evangeline, all about "ye who believe in the beauty and strength of woman's devotion," and a rehash of the tale about faithful Julia waiting for her man. Also included was a reprise of the Sad Farewell. Emmett told the reporter he remembered "how pretty she looked. . . . I sat with my rifle across my knees while she played a tune or two on the organ." An astonishing feat, especially considering that Julia's granddaughter said her grandmother couldn't play a lick on the organ. But then, Emmett was ever given to treacly claptrap: He even delivered himself of a paean of praise for the Condon Bank contingent of Coffeyville bandits, a contribution to the misinforming of an entire generation.

In all my life I have never known an exhibition of chilled steel nerve such as Grat Dalton, Powers, and Broadwell gave there, waiting, watching the minute hand of the big clock on the wall creep slowly around, counting the seconds, while the town armed itself and began bombarding the bank.

This, of course, in spite of the fact that dull-witted Grat and his henchmen could not have watched the "big clock on the wall," or they would have known a bank man was coolly lying to them about the safe being still on its time lock.

Emmett apparently made this speech every time he got somebody who would stand still long enough to listen to it. In late April, 1931, probably on the same trip, he pontificated for the *Dallas Times-Herald*, which called him a "prominent Hollywood realtor," and duly reported his pious remark that "In our ignorance, we thought we were justified." Which translates as, "So long as our hearts were pure, it was all right to kill people and rob them." After the Coffeyville visit, Emmett and Julia went back to California. In the autumn of 1935, they entertained a visitor in their little bungalow on Prince Street in Hollywood. Their caller was none other than Charley Gump, a Coffeyville drayman, who still carried the scar he got from Bob's Winchester slug all those years before. This time the meeting was all peace and pleasant conversation. As the Los Angeles *Evening Herald* reported, Gump stayed to partake of "the tasty roast prepared by Mrs. Dalton, who has been married to the 'grandest man in the world' for the past twenty-seven years."

Gump, full of tasty roast and mellow with years, opined for the press that he didn't really think Bob meant to kill him, but just to "disable me by shooting me through the hand," a mighty charitable—and unlikely— conclusion. He also told the reporters that Emmett "is now one of our best citizens," before he departed into the sunset.

It is somehow fitting that Emmett died in Hollywood, which would later successfully distort the story of Coffeyville out of all resemblance

Mrs. H. W. Dalton, 1889

to what really happened. Broderick Crawford, Brian Donlevy, and Randolph Scott started it all out back in 1940 with *When the Daltons Rode*. The Daltons rode again five years later (sure enough, The Daltons Ride Again), with Lon Chaney Jr. and Milburn Stone (Doc in Gunsmoke), who deserved better.

In 1975 Richard Widmark starred in *The Last Day*, and TV chipped in in 1979 with Jack Palance and Dale Robertson in a thoroughly forgettable drama called *Last Ride of the Dalton Gang*. In between, in 1957, Hollywood produced a dreadful turkey called *The Dalton Girls*, about which the less is said, the better.

Before we leave the mysterious Julia, there is the matter of the Sixth Rider. For many years a dispute has raged about whether the Dalton gang numbered five or six when they rode into Coffeyville. If there were six, there is further dispute about who the "sixth rider" was and what happened to him, and on and on.

I am inclined to believe that there may indeed have been a Sixth Man. The nominees have run the gamut from Bill Doolin—probably the best candidate—to Bittercreek Newcomb, to somebody named Allie Ogee, to, sure enough, Julia Johnson.

It was probably inevitable that Julia got into the Coffeyville mix. After all, what could be more romantic than the frontier woman galloping into danger at the side of her beloved, even if he was a career outlaw? Sadly, it's pretty obvious that the fair Julia wasn't part of the raid. Since she didn't know Emmett at that time, she would be unlikely to go galloping along with an outlaw gang unless her heartthrob was beside her. Anything is possible, of course, but in this writer's opinion, the chances of Julia riding along on the Coffeyville raid are something even less than nil.

Which brings us to the finale: what happened to the Dalton Ladies?

Julia Johnson we know about, since she spent the rest of Emmett's life with him, but the end for Flo is far less clear. There are a couple of sources that have her dying before the raid, probably of cancer, provoking Bob's sorrow and rage. Emmett says Bob found out just before the gang left for Coffeyville.

It may also be, however, that the entire tale of Flo/Tom's death on the eve of Coffeyville is pure invention.

Another writer says Flo didn't die that way after all, but left all memory of the owlhoot trail far behind her, married, and "settled down to a humdrum life." Still another source, however, has her "forming her own gang" after the Daltons crapped out at Coffeyville, but then, "[b]efore long, Flo joined Bob in death. This boldest of the West's lady outlaws went out, like Bob, boots down and six-gun smoking."

Where all this happened—if it did—is also a matter of conjecture. One story has her killed in Wichita in 1893, when a holdup went bad. But according to famous U.S. Deputy Marshal Heck Thomas, Flo was shot down in the course of a holdup someplace around Tombstone, Arizona.

There is also a story that in April of 1896, Oklahoma City lawyer D. C. Lewis, a friend, heard from the lady by letter. She was going west by train, she wrote, but would see him again about Christmas.

She never appeared.

Flo, or Tom King, was a real, live outlaw, not an overblown phony of the likes of Belle Starr. Precisely who she was, and how many of the stories about her true, is lost in the mists of the past. She will remain something of an enigma.

It's more fun that way.

CHAPTER EIGHT

Hot Stuff

Chicago May Churchill

Some of the criminally inclined ladies were robbers; some killed people, for both fun and profit; a third group, the aristocrats of the criminal sisterhood, spun their webs with guile, sweet words, and sex appeal. May Churchill was one of the latter, right at the very top of her profession.

At least she was until she got overconfident, and loved not wisely but too well. Far too well.

May was not what today's bleeding hearts would call "deprived," in some way to be pitied and given things because of her poor family background, national origin, race, religious belief, uncaring mother, a tendency to be overweight, pimples, or whatever. What May wanted she went out and got very efficiently on her own, and she had very few scruples about how she got it. May was an Irish girl, born May Duigan, a long-legged, red-haired lass with memorable eyes—"glowing" somebody called them— who realized early on that Ireland, the land of her birth, was decidedly not the land of her dreams. Accordingly, she stole her mother's small savings, bought a passage to America, the Land of Opportunity, and made the most of it. She was fifteen years old.

Still a youngster, she won a part dancing in a Broadway musical called The Belle of New York, and almost immediately the suitors began to flock around. Leading the pack was a rich young man named Sharp, who finally proposed to May in the middle of the theater dressing room, while the other dancers watched in awe and, no doubt, in envy.

Young Sharp lasted only a few months, until May had extracted a grubstake of some $10,000, a substantial chunk of money back then. She pronounced herself bored with big houses and flocks of servants, and moved into New York's Tenderloin district, then a mecca for high rollers, high-priced mistresses, and rich men on the prowl. She fit right in, and swung into the high life immediately, a vivid picture in high-priced gowns and jewelry, but still somehow "a picture of sweet innocence," according to one description. She was irresistible.

Before long May was expertly juggling the attentions and affections of several wealthy men and their expensive gifts, evading their offers of marriage while still keeping them on the hook. There is some reason to believe that she simply enjoyed watching their devotion and efforts to win her, whether it was from cruelty or simply, as had been suggested, that she didn't like most men.

And then she met the man who would be the guru of her subsequent career. His name was Max Shinborn, and he was a smooth, very successful confidence man-cum-burglar who could well be called the King of the Badgers. Oddly, he seems to have had no particular attraction toward May as a woman, but for some other reason—maybe he admired her talent—he taught her a good deal about his shady trade. Max retired to the Riviera not long after that, having bought a title of nobility (Baron Shindell, he would be), but May, having completed her post-graduate education, was just beginning.

The Badger Game had been around time out of mind, and May played it to the hilt. She would attract a wealthy man (that wasn't hard), invite him to her sumptuous flat (rented, of course), get him into bed (that wasn't hard, either), make love to him, and ply him with drugged champagne. Once he drifted off, May would rifle through his valuables, throw his clothes out the window, and depart.

Upon regaining consciousness, sore-headed and pants-less, the victim would find, instead of his lover, a strange man sitting by the bed staring at him. The stranger had bad news. He grimly told the sucker that while he had been in Dreamland, the lady's irate husband had showed up and dragged her away. He's so angry, said May's confederate, that he intends to call your wife and sue you for every last dime you have.

Chicago May Churchill

But, the stranger added, I can maybe fix things, and I'll try, but it will cost a substantial amount of money. Almost invariably, the flustered pigeon paid up.

May's daring had no bounds. On one occasion, the sucker's check for $5,000 bounced. May's solution was not to write it off as a bad day and a bad debt; instead she went to her pigeon's wealthy father with the check and threatened to sue his wastrel son for fraud. She left with a new check for ten thousand. This one didn't bounce.

May worked her scam in a number of cities, including several in South America after New York got too hot for her, not because she was fleecing men in numbers, but because she managed to get crossways with her protectors, crooked officers of the New York Police. That made the Big Apple an unfavorable business climate and mandated a move elsewhere.

And so, in the late 1890s, May set up shop in Chicago, happy hunting ground for grifters of every kind. May fit right in. The badger game worked wonderfully, and May, ever inventive, even improved upon it. The camera was her new weapon, carefully focused on her bed through tiny holes drilled in the wall. Her camera operators recorded in vivid detail May and her latest pigeon engaged in all sorts of horizontal gymnastics.

When a copy of the film was presented to the sucker, May also presented two options: "They can go into your waste can or to the newspapers," she said matter-of-factly, "I don't care which." Normally, she had no trouble receiving another generous check. And so the good days continued until, in 1900, two of May's partners in crime left Chicago under pressure by the Pinkerton Agency. They went to London, and May decided to give England a try, too.

And so, at the ripe old age of twenty-five, May hit London along with "Kid John" McManus and "Dutch Gus" Miller. They were soon called the "Northumberland Gang." Even though Scotland Yard knew who they were, they proved devilish hard to catch. May turned out to be as good an organizer as she was a siren, and the going was good. A little tact and a few Mickey Finns to put the dupe to sleep worked wonders. One typical strike produced various rings, plus "a lovely horseshoe pin, a diamond-studded watch, and about a thousand pounds" in cash. It was a pretty fair reward for a very short time and almost no effort, and there was much more.

Maybe the wild, dangerous life was beginning to pall on May; maybe she had been "too long at the fair," as the British say, but increasingly she began to turn to opium dreams for solace, sometimes smoking a stupendous twenty or thirty pipes a day. It is a tribute to her enormous willpower that she managed to quit the drug in time. She did not quit her successful racket, however.

The suckers kept coming, and if anything they got even more rewarding. Titled men, men high in the professions, even the son of an earl, fell for May. Her great success moved a high-ranking Scotland Yard officer to call her "the worst woman in London." The Yard would have loved to make a case against May, and maybe that was what moved her to decide to spend some time away in Paris and Vienna before coming back to England.

And then it happened: the biggest event of May's life, and one with far-reaching consequences. In a London joint she ran into old comrade McManus, who introduced her to a friend, a doctor, McManus said.

"Doctor, hell," said May. "I know who you are—you're Eddie Guerin."

The stranger responded affably, "And you're Chicago May."

Now Guerin was an Irishman by way of America, maybe the most famous international jewel thief in history, the real-life Raffles of his day. And something between the two struck sparks, in spite of McManus's sotto voce warning to Guerin that May would take him for every dime—or franc—he had. Guerin was hooked, even though he knew all about his future paramour. In his own words, "Of her moral character the less said the better[;] . . . not only was she a wonton but she was treacherous into the bargain. Many a man, as I was well aware, was even then serving out the last years of his life through her in jails of Europe and America. . . . Yet knowing it, I could not leave her alone. Her beauty held me spellbound."

It was even worse than Guerin thought. The story goes that by that point in her career, May had been the probable cause of five suicides, responsible for the deaths of men she had driven to destruction through shame or bankruptcy.

Now enter "Dutch Gus" again, seeking Guerin with news of what he called "the most beautiful safe in the world," an edifice that resided in the American Express office on the *Rue Scribe* in Paris. It was big and old-fashioned, a good thing to the professional cracksman, and both he and McManus had much experience in that line. Guerin was the master.

Guerin fell in with the plan, and added May, with whom he was then living. She would be the "lookout," he said. The four set up shop in Paris and began to plan. Since the American Express offices acted as a sort of post office for Americans overseas, Guerin covered his reconnaissance visits neatly by simply writing letters to himself in care of American Express and then collecting each one, casting his expert eye over the office and the safe at the same time.

There was just one snag: the building had to be entered without noise, for there was a watchman who lived upstairs. May was the answer, and she found a way to get inside and stay inside simply by going to the office at the close of the business day, pestering the clerks with what she called "inane questions" and, when the opportunity presented itself, hiding under a counter. The clerks, as she said later, "wanting to be rid of me . . . shunted me from one to another."

Once the watchman left the office to prowl upstairs, May unlocked the door for the rest of the gang, who lay in wait until the watchman came back downstairs; they jumped him and tied him up. Guerin and McManus worked on the safe while Miller guarded the watchman and May proceeded to "watch" outside, playing to perfection a most familiar part, a streetwalker looking for her next trick.

It took two hours or so to drill and load the nitroglycerin charge, which Guerin and company fired about two in the morning. There then appeared bad news in the form of a gendarme, who had heard the muffled blast. Since May was the only person in sight, he addressed to her his obvious question: "Where was that explosion, miss?" "Over there," quoth May, pointing in another direction. The policeman left to investigate and did not return.

According to May, that didn't conclude the night's festivities; Guerin and company blew *another* safe in the American Express office about three hours later. May's "work was finished, so I went home to bed."

The burglary had been a huge success. The gang had shoveled heaps of loot into the suitcases they had thoughtfully brought with them, something in the neighborhood of $600,000 in traveler's checks and another $40,000 in currency of several nations. In April 1901, their haul was a king's ransom. Another version of the tale puts the take at a measly $6,000 or so, but that seems to have been only a newspaper guestimate.

May feverishly sewed cash into her coat lining while Guerin filled a trunk with his share. The others had already fled, he said, and they had better do so too. They had already bought tickets on the boat train to Calais and the steamer from there to England. They might well have escaped the armies of French police watching all means of transport had it not been, the story goes, for Guerin's arrogance.

And so, when the couple was walking down the train corridor and met two French officers who questioned them in broken English, Guerin dropped his guard and played le damfool, responding in the beautiful French of which he was so proud. Since the two were posing as British, that was enough to alarm the officers and they put the arm on Eddie. May was allowed to go on to England.

But she could not stay away from her lover, and went back to France, going to see him in prison on the pretense that she was his sister. It was an act of monumental stupidity. Guerin was appalled, and told her to get out, but May could not resist the grand gesture. She wouldn't desert him, she said; he'd need a lawyer, and she tried to give him a handful of money through his cell bars, at which a couple of detectives arrested her.

A disgusted Guerin threw the money into a corner. "Now you've done it, May!" he said, or something like that, and she sure had. Even so, the remark was a bit ungracious, considering that neither one of them would have been in the hands of the flics at all save for his vanity and stupidity on the train.

Guerin and Miller were tried together with May. Both men tried to convince the court that May had nothing to do with the robbery, but there was simply too much evidence against her. Both men were sentenced to life in prison, and not just any prison: it would be French Guiana, so-called Devil's Island. That was tantamount to a death sentence.

May got five years in Montpellier Prison, but she didn't serve it all. Once more, she rolled out her best weapon, seduced the prison doctor, and then blackmailed him into signing a medical release in 1904. Then it was back to England and safety, or at least it would have been had May showed the slightest good sense. She didn't.

For in less than a year, the impossible happened. Guerin not only escaped from Devil's Island, but conned his way to the United States pretending to be part of the staff of a lost archeological expedition. It is said that he blew a few safes in Chicago before running again, this time to England. And so the great reunion came to pass, when May and Guerin met over a beer in the Horse and Groom pub in London.

It didn't last long. The Grand Passion had somehow cooled. The two quarreled, and when Guerin said he'd work alone thereafter, she threatened to send him back to Devil's Island. He persisted and walked out, provoking May to a singularly unladylike rage. She did indeed try her best to send her former lover back to Guiana, but the British government would not do so. So angry did May become that she ill-advisedly laid on an assassination of her former lover. That didn't work either.

May climbed out of a taxi, screaming "shoot him!"—and the shooter did his best. Her chosen assassin was one Charlie Smith, May's current flame and once Eddie's cellmate. It turned out that as a shooter Charlie couldn't hit the ground with his hat even at close range, and Guerin got away with a single bullet wound to the foot. There would be no more, for Smith went crashing down to the pavement under the combined bulk of a constable and several civilians.

His luck didn't get any better, for he got a life sentence for his amateurish attempt. May was sentenced to do fifteen years, and wouldn't get out for twelve. That was in 1918, and she returned to New York.

Things were very different now; the bloom was off the rose. May was getting a bit faded and frumpy, and nobody seemed to care much about her past adventures—or about her. It must have been a bitter pill. Guerin was dead by now; Smith would not be released for five more years. Nobody much wanted to even read her memoirs.

And so May, the woman who had made love to, and ruined, so many men, who had dripped fine jewelry and worn the finest clothing, died alone in a dingy Philadelphia boardinghouse. She was only fifty-three. There was nothing left around her of opulence, nothing to remind her of the great old days.

Except a photograph of Eddie Guerin.

CHAPTER NINE

The Second Belle Starr

Cora Hubbard

Cora wasn't the only outlaw woman to be likened to Belle Starr, at least to Belle as folklore and yellow journalism had created her. Belle was something less than the demonic gang leader the penny dreadfuls—and later the movies—made her out to be. At least to some degree Cora even outdid the storied Belle; at least she was part of one legitimate stickup.

One of Cora's rivals as "the second Belle" was seventeen-year-old May Calvin. She was described as a "notorious horse thief" when in 1893 she was arrested for pinching a pony in Missouri and taking the horse across the border to Kansas. Arrested and returned for trial, she wasn't around Missouri long, departing jail by tunneling through the wall—a hole begun not long before by one Della—or Delia—Oxley, also a horse thief.

May kept it up until the state lost patience and sent her off to the penitentiary. She was quite a sensation according to the newspapers, who rhapsodized about her "luscious" body, "well rounded and plump." The St. Louis Republic called her a "rustic beauty," somewhat unclear in precise meaning, but apparently intended to be a term of great approval.

Her successor, at least according to the papers, was another horse thief, Ethel Smith, or maybe the lady's name was Birdie McCarty, a youngster in her early twenties. She was billed as "the first female horse thief since the palmy days of the reign of May Calvin."

But they were underachievers compared to Cora Hubbard. She was a married woman who lived near Nowata, down in Oklahoma Territory, a very tough lady who conspired with her husband Bud Parker to go a-robbing. They were going to take along Cora's brother and a couple of other losers, hired-hand John Sheets and drifter Whit Tennyson, and go rob the bank at little Pineville. The story goes that all of the men were second-raters, down on their luck, and not great achievers at anything, although Tennyson boasted that he knew all about robbing banks.

Cora's brother drew a diagram of the bank and the planning, such as it was, went forward apace. At the last minute Cora's brother and husband both had second thoughts and backed out of the venture, prompting Cora to remark scathingly that she was through with her husband, because he was a "damn coward." So off Cora went with Sheets and Tennyson to make their fortunes. They stopped long enough in Coffeyville, Kansas, for Sheets to buy a Winchester, and then went on to Weir City to visit Cora's father, once a miner.

He was apparently appalled to see his precious daughter with her hair cut short and wearing men's clothing, in the company of two obvious scumbags, but, as he later said, Cora was a "motherless girl," and he couldn't turn her away. So he sheltered the three for a few days until they rode off to bust their bonanza at Pineville, some sixty miles away.

Cora seems to have been the appointed horse-holder, while the two men bulled into the bank, pushed people around, and walked out of the bank with a little under $600. They also were small-souled enough to steal one man's $15 watch. They stole a horse from a boy they met on the road out of town and rode on into Indian Territory. So far, so good, but behind them a posse was quickly forming; the good citizens of Pineville were on the hunt.

The three tyro bandits ran head-on into a citizens' ambush, in which both Tennyson and Sheets absorbed some citizen buckshot and Cora had her revolver shot out of her hand. The three fled, Tennyson separated from Cora and Sheets. The posse found Tennyson's horse, grazing alone but without her bridle, and the next day the pursuers got word of a man who had paid for lunch with pennies. The posse followed up and found Tennyson, wounded, clanking with deadly weapons, and carrying $120 and change.

Tennyson proved to be a weak reed, and promptly implicated Cora and Sheets. A female bandit was automatically big news, and delighted the newspapers. Cora was instantly compared to Belle Starr, and at least one paper likened her also to Kate Bender, femme fatale of the murderous Bender family, which had done in something between ten and forty travelers in southeast Kansas.

Meanwhile, Cora and Sheets had reached Parsons, Kansas, whence Cora made for her father's home. Sheets was supposed to follow quickly, and the two would then escape to someplace in Iowa. They didn't make it, for Cora was arrested at her father's house and transported to Joplin, Missouri, where—legend has it—a posse man bought her some shoes and stockings, which she promptly put on "without any special display of modesty."

A further search of her father's homestead turned up more money, buried with the tomatoes and potatoes, and a Colt .45 revolver with "Bob Dalton" etched on the grip. It had seven notches carved close to the trigger guard as well, and the papers had a field day with the assumed connection with the leader of the Dalton gang, now extinct. Cora had done good deal of bragging about riding the owlhoot trail with the Dalton gang, and the pistol was said to be proof.

Any connection with the Daltons is tenuous at best, and probably illusory. Anybody can engrave a revolver, but any engraving or carving was sure not done by Bob, at least not honestly, because, by 1892, the year he died at Coffeyville, he is highly unlikely to have killed that many people.

And then, in the midst of all the hoo-ha surrounding the arrest of the "second Belle Starr," John Sheets drove up to the Hubbard home in a buggy, amazed to find a flock of officers instead of the safe haven he expected. Promptly arrested, he joined his cohorts in jail, and ultimately in the courtroom.

Cora took to the public fascination like a duck to water, posing for photographs holding a rifle—presumably unloaded—and wearing the same man's clothing she'd worn during the holdup itself. There was never any real doubt about the guilt of the three, and all were convicted of bank robbery. Cora and Sheets got twelve years apiece and Tennyson ten.

Cora got out of prison on the first day of January 1905. The event was reported, of course, but it seems a little of the excitement was gone from the story of the "second Belle Starr." One paper was ungracious enough to comment on her "greasy dark complexion."

The not-so-appetizing Cora had her hour in the sun. But, just as quickly as she appeared, she faded from the scene. Belle Starr she wasn't.

CHAPTER TEN

The Bobbed-Hair Bandit

Cecilia Clooney

The *really* tough gangster women didn't come along nearly as often as their male counterparts, but when they did, they were a holy terror, at least as tough as the men. Cecilia Clooney was the real thing, a short-lived comet, a streak of terrifying light across the safe world of the ordinary, a lady who left a lot of frightened people in her wake.

It's a wonder Cecilia grew up at all. She was one of eight kids raised—if that's the word—in a New York slum, with intervals in foster homes and orphanages. She and her siblings subsisted on whatever was remotely edible in other people's garbage, and, at least for a while, slept in a coal bin. As if that were not enough to turn any kid into an adult misanthrope, an episode when she was twelve would have left scars that never went away.

It seems an aunt took her in, fed her, and dressed her in what was probably the first pretty dress she'd ever had. When her excuses for parents found out, they pulled her back home, where the pretty dress was exchanged for the usual rags and then sold. As if that were not enough to warp a kid's spirit, two years later she was farmed out to a brush factory at about $3 a week. She started whoring at about fifteen, worked as a laundress for a while, and finally was married at twenty.

There was no public dole in those far-off days, no benevolent governmental agency to watch over people in hopeless trouble. If they were ever to change their lot, it was up to them.

Pregnant, her husband Ed unemployed, the two youngsters contemplated suicide, and even went so far as to acquire a gun with which to take their own lives—and then came inspiration. They had no love for the society that had turned its back and left them behind; why not use their new revolver to get some back? Why not go and rob the world that had treated them so badly?

They pulled their first job early in January, 1924, sticking up a store to the tune of almost $700, more money by far than either of them had ever seen. They fled on foot, of course; penniless bandits can't afford getaway cars. They bought a few little luxuries for themselves, and carefully preserved half of the loot for their unborn child.

They were careful with their spending, but that initial success simply whetted their appetites for more. Cecilia had held the gun on store personnel and customers during their first holdup, and she did so again when they stuck up an A & P store for a little over a hundred dollars. This time, however, she held two guns.

That same day, the couple walked a few blocks and relieved a merchant of $250, and a week later hit two more stores for smaller amounts. Their two-person crime wave, fairly minor so far, inevitably caught the fancy of the press, and Cecilia became "the bobbed-haired bandit." Where mob molls and female swindlers and such were familiar newspaper fare, two-gun girl bandits didn't come along every day.

Meanwhile, Cecilia and Ed continued to build up their baby's account, and now began to buy some luxury items for themselves. Thus it was that on the 22nd of January Cecilia was wearing a sealskin coat when she walked into a grocery store and asked the proprietor what was in a barrel. "Herring," he said, and Cecilia asked him to open it to check the freshness of the contents; when he did so he looked up into the bore of her automatic.

"Stick up your hands and keep quiet," she is quoted as saying, "or I'll fill you full of lead" or something equally disquieting. "That's a nice little boy," said she, and herded him into the back room. There she looted his pockets of more than $600, mostly in checks; Ed, meanwhile, had cleaned out the cash register; he is said to have given some advice to a woman customer who walked in during the robbery: "Shut up and get in the back room or I'll kill you," which seemed plain enough. The lady sensibly obeyed.

So the Bobbed-Haired Bandit had struck again, and the papers loved it. The police did not, and one source says that over 500 officers and detectives were assigned to run her down. Well, maybe, but the Brooklyn police must have had a lot of other crimes to solve as well, and committing half a thousand officers to catch one small-time bandit could well be termed over-reaction.

However many officers went searching for Cecilia and Ed, they first needed to sort out who they were looking for, and the witnesses didn't agree: she was short, said some; no, she wasn't, said others, she was tall. The police captain commanding the search said he thought she "consorts with bandits at night and probably lives respectably during the daytime." That was pretty close to accurate, although so far her only criminal consort had been Ed.

The work of putting away women with short hair went on apace. It was complicated by the appearance of other bobbed-haired bandits, and by the appearance of a couple of morons dressed up in bobbed-hair wigs and short skirts. They went into the police bag, it is said, because, being both male and unpracticed, they were unable to run from the police in high heels.

While Cecilia and Ed added to their unborn child's stash and spoiled themselves a little, the public was fascinated, the papers were enchanted. Consider this epic in the staid *New York Times*: "Who is the Bobbed-Haired Bandit? Who are her people? Nobody knows who she is. She may be a he. She may be two or three or any number of hardy young adventuresses. But one thing is certain: after only a few weeks of rapid and efficient pillaging, she is already a tradition, the symbol of a reckless age."

And so what had begun as a quest for pocket-money and some measure of small-time revenge had turned into a cause *célèbre*.

But Cecilia and Ed were getting disgusted. So much competition was bringing more police into the hunt and more and more small business people were arming themselves. New York was getting too hot, the baby was coming, and it was time to run; the couple began to think about one big strike to fund their departure.

The hiding place they chose was Jacksonville, Florida. To finance their retirement, they decided, they would knock over nothing less than huge Nabisco, which Ed had heard had lots of cash receipts. No doubt. But getting at it took some planning, and part of the plot concerned their means of escape. This, they thought, was best accomplished by hiring a limousine, complete with driver. After all, who could possibly suspect the dignified occupants of such an expensive, high-class vehicle?

And so Ed and Cecelia registered at a good hotel as Mr. and Mrs. Parker of Boston. They rented their limo and driver, and took a test ride around town. Next morning was D-Day. This time, their ride took them through a park, where Ed turned the hapless driver into a prisoner, bound and gagged on the floor in the back seat. Cecelia amused herself by pushing one of her high-heeled shoes into the driver's neck, "and then I pressed the heel down a little, but not enough to hurt him."

The operation had gone well so far, but now things started coming unstuck. They parked the limo, threatened the driver with death if he moved, and went inside, seeking the manager's office. Once there, they pulled their weapons and lined up and bullied a number of office staff. Cecelia held her familiar two pistols on the staff, while Ed ransacked the office, throwing papers and files in all directions, seeking their bonanza.

Curses! Foiled again! For Ed found not one thin dime. The safe was open, but it was empty. Ed the master criminal didn't realize that the sack just beneath the safe held almost $6,000, ready for the bank.

And then their day really fell apart, as a bank man tried to grab Cecelia's gun; the attempt failed, and in the scuffle that followed she fired a wild shot, hitting nobody. She then drove the bank employee and another man into a back room, bashing them with the pistol, and slammed the door.

Enter Ed, the mental giant. Furious that anybody had resisted his wife, he drove two bullets blindly through the door, hitting twice the employee who had tried to grab Cecelia's weapon. There was nothing left to do but run, driven by the knowledge that if Ed had killed anybody, the electric chair would now be waiting for them.

They did get to Jacksonville, however, safe for the moment but almost stone broke. It was back to one furnished room again, and within a week the baby arrived, a girl. The child was ill and had no chance, dying five days later. The couple, now completely out of money, had to lie to a local undertaker to even get the baby buried—we're expecting money from home, they said, and the undertaker responded, very likely out of simple kindness.

Ed and Cecelia were the only people at the little girl's burial.

Ed didn't dare even look for work, for the couple had made another of their bone-headed errors. It was Cecelia's blunder this time, for she had mindlessly carried a small address book on the morning of the Nabisco holdup. It was gone, dropped in the Nabisco office, and the police had it, and now their full descriptions were everywhere, including pictures. Now it was only a matter of time.

And time ran out on the 21st of April, when two New York officers burst into their room. They faced the officers with guns drawn, their hands shaking with hunger. "It ain't worth it," said one detective, and Cecelia agreed and threw her pistol on the bed. Ed followed suit.

At least now the two fugitives could eat, and they did, eating everything in sight in the train diner taking them back to New York. The papers had another big story, and the inevitable questions followed: Why did young Cecelia end up a criminal? "We didn't want our baby born in a furnished room," she said. And maybe that was really the truth after all.

They each got ten to twenty for the ten armed robberies with which they were charged and went off to their separate prisons with pious, tearful assurances that they would be together again. Cecelia left a legacy, too, a bit of paper she asked the trial judge to pass to the newspapers: "To those girls who think they would like to see their names in the papers as mine has been, or think they would like to do what I have done, let me say: Don't try to do it; you don't know what you suffer. While I smile, my heart is breaking in me."

Then she and Ed were gone up the river for the next six long years, and when they were released their lives had yet another obstacle to deal with: Ed had lost an arm in a machine-shop accident up at Sing Sing; his days at heavy labor—all he knew—were finished. But the real miracle was that the two had survived all the hardship and the prison years.

There was one bright spot, however; Ed had received a payment of $12,000 from the state of New York for the loss of his arm, and that sufficed to buy a small farm up-state. There they settled down at last in something approaching peace, and even produced another child.

This one lived.

CHAPTER ELEVEN

A Greek Tragedy

Bonnie Parker

Across the fields of yesterday
she sometimes comes to me,
a little girl just back from play,
the girl I used to be.
And yet she smiles so wistfully,
once she has crept within;
I wonder if she hopes to see,
the woman I might have been.

Blanche Barrow wrote this little poem about herself in about 1933, but it also fit precisely her more famous sister-in-law.

As a girl, Bonnie Parker never had much to be proud of or excited about. For her the world was strictly black-and-white; there wasn't any Technicolor, and no prospect of seeing any. That was for other people. Her bricklayer father died when she was still tiny, and her mother eked out a living for Bonnie and her siblings as a seamstress in a Dallas suburb with the uninviting name of Cement City.

Bonnie was a tiny blond, ninety pounds or so and moderately attractive, but nobody's beauty. She had a pretty fair brain, however, once she had a chance to really use it; in school she won prizes in public speaking, spelling, and writing. Today, she might well have had a chance at a scholarship to attend college; in the Dallas of 1930, that was unlikely. In that year she was nineteen, and working as a waitress at a place called Marco's Cafe. She had no prospects, nothing to dream about.

In a curious touch of fate, one of her regular restaurant customers was a post office employee named Ted Hinton, who would later become a Dallas deputy sheriff. They would meet again.

But for now, Bonnie could see nothing else in her future but hard work and poverty. To make things worse, she was married to a real dead end. His name was Ray Thornton, by profession an outlaw, and he would never hang around home much; he was doing ninety-nine years for murder. Bonnie doesn't seem to have been grieving overmuch. The story goes that she had kept several men on the hook even before Thornton went up the river. Still, it was at best a humdrum existence, and unlikely to get any better.

But then along came Clyde Barrow. Just what Bonnie saw in him remains a mystery. Clyde was not all that bright, certainly Bonnie's intellectual inferior, and a psychopath to boot. But Bonnie wanted something better out of life; although Clyde wasn't it, maybe he meant excitement to her, a flash of fire in the gloom of her dreary life.

And so the two went a-robbing together, dinky nickel-and-dime jobs. They stuck up mom-and-pop grocery stores and service stations and neighborhood banks and stole cars until Clyde was captured in March of 1930 and sent off to prison, where he spent the next two years. While there he resisted another inmate's repeated sexual assaults by killing the man.

Clyde came out of the slammer with what some historians describe as a mighty case of resentment toward society. It may well have had something to do with what had happened to him while in prison, or at least he said it did when plotting "revenge" against the Texas penitentiary system. But of course he blamed society and the prison authorities and other cons for whatever it was. Like other punks time out of mind, he wouldn't accept responsibility for any of the misery he caused himself. A fellow inmate said prison had changed him "from a schoolboy to a rattlesnake." Maybe he rattled some to start with.

With Clyde out of the pen, it was back to robbing people, this time in company not only with Bonnie, but also with his brother Buck and Buck's wife, Blanche. The two-bit crime wave they created went as planned until, in July of 1933, Blanche was captured, her vision badly impaired by splinters of glass blown out of a car's back window by a lawman's weapon in a wild shootout in Platte City, Missouri. Buck was mortally wounded in the same fracas.

So their crime wave went on, and every police officer in a dozen states searched for them. The worst of it wasn't so much the robberies, for their largest score from any bank was something around $1,500; it was the killing. For in their criminal odyssey the "Barrow Gang," as they had come to be called, left fifteen dead people in their wake, most of them police officers.

Their trail of murders has been ascribed to a contempt for the law, to hatred of all peace officers, to some sort of thrill in defying authority, or even to all of these. Maybe so. Maybe not. Or perhaps it was that both of them were sociopaths, empty people, so that to them other humans didn't matter any more than a cigarette pack in the gutter. Or maybe, probably, it somehow made them feel superior to other people and forget their own shortcomings.

If that was the motivation, it helps explain their fascination with photographs. They were not ordinary photos, either, but mostly tough poses holding various firearms, lots of them, like the famous photo of Bonnie with a cigar clutched in her teeth holding, as usual, a revolver. She smoked in fact, but never cigars, and later was at some pains to make that clear.

After his release, Clyde armed himself to the teeth, his favorite weapon the military's reliable BAR—Browning Automatic Rifle—with which he equipped himself by simply breaking into National Guard Armories. Bonnie is said to have used a BAR in at least one police shootout, but little is known of her preferences otherwise.

The two of them did not run alone. An early recruit was W. D. Jones, a Barrow family friend, who was all of sixteen when he invited himself along as a student criminal. That was Christmas Eve of 1932, and that very next night he and Clyde killed a police officer. He was not the only recruit: Raymond Hamilton and Roy Methven, both professional hoodlums, were early members, as were Buck and Blanche Barrow.

Clyde, leader of the pack, repeatedly demonstrated his intellectual poverty. In one hideout, for example, they were given away by loud parties—"we bought a case of beer a day" according to Bonnie—and by Barrow's careless discharge of a BAR round into the ceiling.

Still, Bonnie stuck to her creepy, murderous boyfriend, even though she seemed conscious that they were on the road to hell by the shortest route. She even wrote poetry about it, how the two of them would "go down together" in a sort of blazing Götterdämmerung. But it didn't stop Bonnie, and it hurt a lot of other people. In one shootout in Joplin, Missouri, they killed two officers; and Bonnie is known to have sprayed BAR slugs at another lawman who was saved by a sturdy tree from all but flying wood splinters.

Constantly on the move, they covered the whole midsection of America, robbing banks and other establishments from Texas to Minnesota, stealing cars, kidnapping the owners of at least one of them, and killing another man. Perpetually on the run, they were reduced to living rough, cooking over open fires, sleeping on the ground. As the high life got tougher along the way, Jones decided he'd had enough and departed in one of the cars he'd helped steal.

It got worse. Clyde managed to run the car off the road in Texas during one of their endless drives, passing warning signs for a bridge under construction, and ending up in a depression next to the road. He didn't suffer from his own mistake, but Bonnie did.

Nobody is now sure whether something in the car caught fire, or if the battery spilled acid into the passenger compartment; but whatever it was, it cost Bonnie disabling and very painful third-degree burns on one leg. The leg muscles contracted so that it was almost impossible for her to walk. She had either to hop and drag one foot, or be carried by Barrow.

A temporary halt to rest in an Arkansas hideout was cut short when Buck Barrow and Jones fouled up a holdup and killed still another officer in the process. They moved on to what they thought would be a safe haven over in western Missouri, the Red Crown Tourist Court in Platte City, where at least Bonnie could rest and get some sort of treatment.

The gang proceeded to fumble that chance, too. Blanche Barrow paid the rent and food bill in coins, of all things, and registered just three people as guests, when the proprietor could clearly see five. Not content with those blunders, the gang made the mother and father of all mistakes

Bonnie Parker and Clyde Barrow
WESTERN HISTORY COLLECTIONS, UNIVERSITY OF OKLAHOMA LIBRARIES

when they taped newspapers over their room windows. Then Clyde and Jones went into town to buy, among other things, atropine sulphate for Bonnie's leg.

Since the law had spread the word to watch for people buying this drug, and local officers had also heard of the gang's strange doings at the motel, a posse soon showed up at the Red Crown and a firefight followed. The gang got away in the end, but Buck Barrow had taken a vicious head wound, and his wife had glass fragments in both eyes.

Next stop was Dexfield Park, an abandoned amusement park up in Iowa. Citizen suspicion was aroused by the bloody bandages adorning the gang, and still another firefight followed. Buck died in the hospital a few days later. Blanche went to jail.

Bonnie and Clyde and Jones ran for it yet again.

In January of 1933, Clyde managed the escape of Methven and Hamilton and several others from the same Texas prison where he had languished. He must have felt it was the ultimate triumph over the forces that had "oppressed him" all his worthless life.

It was at last the "revenge" he had babbled about so often, and in the process still another lawman was very badly wounded. It was also the last straw for the law. And so the state of Texas sent in the first team, the best man they could find, an extraordinary Ranger named Frank Hamer.

Over a long career, Hamer was credited with fifty-three kills in the line of duty; along the way, it was said, he had also been wounded a total of seventeen times. If any man could manage to take Bonnie and Clyde out of circulation, it was surely Hamer. He was one tough cookie, a single-minded bulldog in the famous tradition of the young Ranger who arrived by train to quell a riot alone, with only his saddle and rifle. When asked why the Rangers had sent only a single man, the youngster is said to have replied, "Ain't but one riot, is there?" Hamer was exactly that kind of man.

And then, on Easter Sunday of 1934, the gang killed two young highway patrol troopers. The event produced a fresh crop of stories about the gang, some of it apparently invention by an "eyewitness" who wasn't. One of the most horrifying was the tale of Bonnie laughing at the way one officer's head "bounced like a rubber ball" as she shot him, and she and Barrow were said to have done the shooting.

The tale was at least in part discredited later. Methven, at the time part of the gang, said he fired the first shot. He also said Bonnie advanced on the two officers "to help them" after they had been shot down by the rest of the gang. This last tale is a little dubious, as Bonnie, as bad as she felt, was in all likelihood neither shooting nor helping, but probably asleep in the back seat of the gang's car. The same incident produced the equally dubious story that lawmen found at the scene a cigar bearing "tiny teeth marks," presumably Bonnie's.

A reward announcement for the highway patrol murders offered $1,000 for Bonnie and Clyde—just the corpses, mind you, not living bodies—and Hamer was going to do his considerable best to oblige. Texas governor "Ma" Ferguson, who otherwise spent a part of her career turning professional cons loose on society, pledged another thousand.

And then in May 1934, the law at last got lucky. The formidable Hamer had been tracking Clyde since February, carefully plotting his movements, learning what made him tick. Barrow was very good at playing the "state line" game, dodging back and forth over state borders when pursuing officers from one state got too close. But even at this he set a pattern, which Hamer saw and followed, until he was very close to his quarry.

The final act was played out on the morning of May 23, 1934. Hamer and five other officers had lain in ambush along a road during the night, including Ted Hinton, Bonnie's old customer at the café. They were almost ready to close down their stakeout when they hit pay dirt. They heard the engine of a Ford V-8 approaching at high speed, until it roared into view and then stopped or slowed at the sight of Methven's father by the side of the road. The elder Methven was a Hamer plant, and he did his job well. Bonnie and Clyde slowed or stopped, and the lawmen opened up on them.

The lawmen's fusillade was devastating, starting with the roar of BARs, thoughtfully procured by the great state of Texas at Hamer's request. Each of the six lawmen opened up on the outlaws' car with automatic rifle fire—armor-piercing bullets—then shifted over to shotgun rounds, and finished with pistols. If this seems to be overkill, it's well to remember all the bodies Bonnie and Clyde left behind them, many of them peace officers.

There is little question that Hamer and his men did not spend much time shouting pointless commands like "Halt, police!" There is a story that Hamer intended to challenge, but one of the other officers opened fire without waiting for Hamer to yell at their quarry. In the end, there was apparently no challenge at all; nor did it matter much, for this was the heart of a vicious gang that had killed a lot of people, most of them officers of the law.

When the shooting died away, the car—stolen, of course—was a piece of junk, and Bonnie and Clyde were little better. Each had more than fifty bullet wounds, or maybe it was a total of fifty between them, depending on the source you read. The coroner settled for seventeen wounds on Barrow's body and twenty-six on Bonnie's.

One thing was for sure, they were was very dead. They had not fired a shot.

In the Ford was the usual Barrow equipment: an arsenal of handguns, thousands of rounds of ammunition, and the usual BARs. There were also fifteen sets of license plates from several states in the bullet-riddled sedan.

Hamer's feat was a sensation. Whether you thought Bonnie and Clyde were Romeo and Juliet or a stench in the nostrils of honest people, chances are you read every one of the thousands of words the newspapers churned out about them. Before the ambush site could be cleared, people appeared to grab whatever they could as souvenirs. Locks of Bonnie's hair and pieces of her dress were particular favorites, and one man was barely stopped from carving off one of Clyde's ears with his pocket knife.

The car, bodies and all, was towed to nearby Arcadia, Louisiana, where Conger's furniture store and funeral parlor took over. The town of some two thousand abruptly acquired an estimated ten thousand more bodies, provisions sold out, beer prices almost doubled, and a general carnival atmosphere prevailed.

And here also a curious sort of irony came to pass. A young man from a nearby town who'd once been kidnapped by the gang was called to Arcadia to identify the bodies. During the kidnapping, Bonnie had asked him what he did for a living, and he'd told her he was an undertaker. "Maybe you'll be working on me," she said lightly. And sure enough, he was asked to stay on and help the local undertaker with the embalming.

Bonnie was buried in Dallas, her funeral a huge event attracting some twenty thousand people, almost crowding out her parents. Flowers poured in from everywhere, including some purporting to come from John Dillinger and Pretty Boy Floyd, although this story sounds very much like urban legend. The biggest bunch of all, however, came from the newsboys of Dallas, where the outlaws' end had sold half a million papers.

Bonnie's headstone is the final irony. No doubt its inscription came from her parents, who remembered her as they thought she was, not as she ended. It's worth repeating:

As the flowers are all made sweeter,
By the sunshine and the dew,
So this old world is made brighter,
By the lives of folks like you.

I guess that doesn't include the relatives and friends of the dead she and Clyde left along their back trail.

⚊ ⚊

The funerals were over by the end of May, but the big-time criminal news was just beginning. Law enforcement was getting better and better—for one thing, more and more police vehicles had two-way radios—and that year the string ran out for more and more of the big names of crime. Dillinger was killed the next July, dead as a doornail in a Chicago street; and that fall, both Baby Face Nelson and Pretty Boy Floyd followed him to the Great Beyond.

Bonnie has her apologists and always will, especially those who lament that Hamer didn't give the two a chance to surrender. Then there is a group that says well, gosh, she really wasn't all that bad; there's no proof she really shot anybody. Well, maybe, but the fact remains that Bonnie was at least an accomplice in eight murders, seven kidnappings, and a multitude of armed robberies and other crimes, all of which made her eligible for the death penalty in Texas as a habitual criminal.

In the end, maybe Bonnie Parker got lucky at last on that dusty Louisiana road.

CHAPTER TWELVE

The Rose of the Cimarron

Rosa Dunn

There is much mystery in the events of the past, especially the very distant past, which is one thing that makes it especially fascinating. No matter how well chronicled, there is always a part missing or something that ought to be there but isn't. It is worse still to find a remarkable event or a special person and then discover that no two chronicles can agree about that event or person.

So it is with the Rose of the Cimarron, a woman who appears prominently in tales of the Doolin gang and their violent times. But she is somehow seen through a glass darkly, or as an image vastly different from what you would expect to see. The Rose is not something from a morality play, but at the same time there is something about her you cannot quite touch.

There is general agreement that she started life as Rosa—or maybe Rose—Dunn, one of several children of a family from Cowley, Kansas, born back in 1878. She was luckier than most girls of her time—she got a superior education in a Catholic school. Her stepfather was a doctor, but her favorite family member was probably her brother Dee, who was a rancher of sorts; she would sometimes stay at his ranch.

Rose is described as having "a gypsy-like beauty . . . thin and dark with blue-black hair that hung to her shoulders. Her skin was flawless with the look of a golden tan."

Now Dee's friends were not the sort of people Rosa's parents would have chosen for her, or at least not all of them were. Some of them ran

Rose of the Cimarron, sweetheart of George Newcombe, a member of the Dalton and Doolin Gangs

with the Doolin gang, who started out as rustlers. Dee fenced some of the stolen stock for them, and his ranch was always a safe haven when they were on the run from the law. In all probability Rosa met a few of them when she visited her brother.

The trouble with reconstructing Rose's "outlaw days" is that at nineteen she married a solid citizen named Nobel—or Noble—who dug wells and did some blacksmithing for a living. That marriage lasted thirty-plus years until his death, when Rose remarried. The problem with Rose's story lies in the tangled semi-factual outlaw history that has grown up around her.

The story goes that along about 1893 a very young and nubile Rosa fell deeply in love with Doolin gang mainstay Bitter Creek Newcomb, so-called, it is said, by his frequent repetitions of a song of the time, "I'm a wild wolf from Bitter Creek, and it's my night to howl." Maybe so; at least the appellation stuck with him until he didn't need it any more, being dead.

Anyhow, the real story of Rosa opens when she went to see her boyfriend at his boarding house, the City Hotel in Ingalls, Oklahoma. The City was not only the only two-story building in town, but a sort of social center, since the proprietor, Mary Pierce, in the words of a contemporary lawman, "always kept three or four girls around and spent all her waking hours planning new diversions for her guests."

The law knew all about the Doolin gang's fondness for Ingalls, quiet, discreet, and off the beaten path. And this fine morning a posse was closing in on Ingalls to abate the Doolin nuisance. One story tells that it was Rosa's sharp eyes that saw them creeping into the town and gave the alarm. There are other tales of how the outlaws were alerted, including an alarm given by a young boy, but what followed was a monumental firefight.

And a monumental tale of love, daring, and physical agility. Once the battle started, Rosa was on the top story of the hotel and Bitter Creek was down in the street, fighting with only his Colt. Then he was wounded, and fell to the ground, his revolver empty. Rosa, says outlaw legend, grabbed her lover's rifle and cartridge bandoleer, quickly made a rope of strips torn from bed sheets, and climbed down it to the street.

Now picture this dainty young woman somehow balancing both rifle and cartridge belt, or maybe lowering them ahead of her, and then climbing down behind them. Picture her then shinnying down the outside of the building on bed sheets through a wild gunfight.

Here she either got her lover a horse and helped him mount and then got up behind him, or maybe it was in front of him. Or in another version she boosted him onto the horse, slapped the horse on the fanny, and sent him off to safety. In yet another iteration of the tale, Rosa not only helped him mount and get clear, but also nursed him back to health. Not long after that, however, brother Bee (or Dee) Dunn and his brother blew Bitter Creek into the next world in their role of part-time bounty-hunters.

People around Ingalls at the time of the battle either said Bitter Creek didn't have a girl at all, or said Rosa Dunn was far away from town at the time of the fight, visiting her brother on his ranch. In spite of disagreement as to Rosa's role at the Ingalls battle—if any—her legend grew apace. It even produced some truly sloppy poetry, like this:

> Shadows of dead men stand by the wall,
> Watching the fun of the pioneer ball;
> Rose of the Cimarron, Bitter Creek's girl,
> Stood watching the dancers glide and whirl;
> The dance grows wilder; they're young, you see;
> Gosh, said Red Buck, so were we.

Red Buck, by the way, was Red Buck Waightman, one of the truly vile criminal dirt bags in the history of the West. The only logical reason for him to have been mentioned in that sweet poesy of love is that his name makes for better meter than Bitter Creek.

In all probability the tale of the Rose of the Cimarron owes its existence to the perceived need for some romantic interest when the film *Passing of the Oklahoma Outlaws* was in production. Bill Tilghman, a fine officer and an honest man, was often asked about the identity of the Rose, and his answer was generally to this effect: "Oh, just an outlaw's girl, who finally married a good man and reared a fine family. I cannot reveal her identity."

What happened to Rosa Dunn is as cloaked in mystery as what role she had in the outlaw doings of the Doolin gang. Even her appearance is not exactly known. Western writer James Horan described her as "slim and graceful as a doe . . . Oklahoma's most desperate woman." At the time of writing that, Horan said "there was evidence" that she was the wife of "one of Oklahoma's prominent men," and "mother of beautiful children," but that's as far as Horan chose to go. He added that only seven men, sworn to silence, had known her secret.

The Dunn family is said to have been a respected one, but Rose's brothers were not above a bit of rustling in addition to their ranching and bounty-hunting endeavors. And it is said the Rose, as a kid, was not above helping her brothers drive rustled stock to a compliant butcher. How she met Newcomb is no longer known—maybe at one of the neighborhood dances, where, it is said, Doolin himself did the fiddling.

Bitter Creek and fellow outlaw Charley Pierce were ushered into the Great Beyond by the Dunn boys in the spring of 1895. One version of their demise says they were shot down in front of the Dunn ranch on their way to "visit Rose." The bounty was several thousand dollars per outlaw, a great deal of money in that far-off day. The fact that her brothers blew poor old Bitter Creek into eternity for the reward, not surprisingly moved Rosa to swear she'd never speak to them again, or so the story goes.

What happened to Rosa after that is not clear. One version of her later life says she married one Charles Albert Noble, a local politician, had some children, and died at the ripe old age of seventy-six in Washington State. Another has her marrying a well-known Oklahoma politician; it may be the same man, but this source delicately omits his name for the better preservation of the Rose's privacy and reputation.

The legends move on from there, with Rosa marrying various people and living happily ever after. They are all great stories, but sadly there are several holes in the scenario: the first is that in all probability Rosa wasn't anywhere near Ingalls on the day of the great battle—at least, nobody could remember seeing her there; and Ingalls was no more than a wide spot in the road. Certainly had a nubile lass shinnied down a hotel wall carrying weapons, the chances are pretty fair that the picture would stick in somebody's mind; it's not what you see every day.

Another sad part of this romantic tale is the famous picture of Rosa, now romantically called the Rose of the Cimarron. It shows a pensive, attractive young woman, caressing a big revolver; why shore, that's what tough young outlaw women do; trouble is, it ain't Rosa.

The great lawman Bill Tilghman was part of the combine that made and promoted *The Passing of the Oklahoma Outlaws.* In those days, moviemakers might publish a little book you could buy when you saw the film, and for the book you needed pictures. Nobody had one of the Rose of the Cimarron—and probably nobody cared about having one of the real woman—so a model had to be found.

The lady chosen was resident in jail at the time and probably never heard of The Rose, but she was given the gun—presumably unloaded—and sat demurely for a photo that would have a lasting place in American outlaw mythology. Her reward, one story says, was a reduction in sentence and, although nobody knew it at the time, a species of immortality.

Whatever the truth about the Rose of Cimarron legend, it's hard to beat: beauty, true love, courage, adventure, tragedy, battle; it's all there. Such stories will not permit of debunking, even if it's possible. Undimmed by time—or truth, for that matter—the tale of the Rose of the Cimarron will be around forever.

CHAPTER THIRTEEN

Vicious

Ma Staffleback

It is, or used to be, an old miners' maxim that "a mine is only an expensive hole in the ground," and there's a good deal of truth to that expression. As every miner knows, most of those holes are simply empty space, for mining is a chancy business.

Out in Galena, however, it was different. Galena was a wide spot in the road out in southeastern Kansas, about four miles north of the Oklahoma line and just west of the Missouri border. The land was not prime for farming, but in the late nineteenth century it was sitting on a world of lead and zinc. In the 1870s, 1880s, and 1890s, it blossomed into a boomtown of some thirty thousand inhabitants, and at its peak in the 1890s it was producing something like a quarter of all the lead and zinc in the entire world. There were some three hundred holes in the ground, lots of them working shafts, some abandoned and filling with water.

Galena ate up at least two nearby small competitors, and by 1910 the town counted an opera house, three newspapers, and the same number of banks. The riches of Galena required lots of men: miners, hoistmen, carpenters, haulers, framers, sawmill hands—and of course, virtually all these men were young and single. They worked hard and when their shifts were done they had need to play. That fact virtually mandated certain age-old municipal requirements: restaurants, saloons, and whorehouses, with all of which Galena was well equipped.

The night was one long tumult, what with the regular racket of booze-fueled celebration punctuated by gunfire and the crash of furniture as some dispute resolved itself with death or injury to one or more celebrants. In fact, those citizens involved with law enforcement or the healing arts—and funeral undertaking—tried to sleep as much as possible during the day, the better to face the long night of murder, mayhem, miscellaneous violence, and general chaos.

The Galena *Sentinel* put it pretty well:

> *The boys were high rollers in those days. Red Hot Street was the main thoroughfare and the scene of bloody action. Along this street were clustered haunts of dissipation and prostitution. The most frequented places were the Round Top, the Hickory Tree, the Log Cabin, and Dick Swapp's Place. In saloons the lewd and the reckless were congregated at all hours, intoxicated by wine, lulled . . . by siren's charms to commit deeds undreamed of under other circumstances.*

Among the men and women who created this chaos and profited from it was one Ma Steffleback, or Stafflebach, or Staffleback—people spelled it several ways—who can safely be described as a hollow woman driven almost entirely by greed. She ran a house staffed with adept and willing ladies of the evening, but she also had a grim sideline.

Ma lived with a man named Wilson, to whom she may or may not have been married, and had several sons who shared the maternal fondness for money and contempt for the law and other people. Ma's offspring had already seen a good deal of local jails for relatively minor crimes; now they were about to follow their mother into the big time.

Ma's recipe for success was simple: when a high-roller with a bulging poke appeared in her house, he might be selected as her next investment. If so, the first step was to get him well and truly drunk, or drug him, whichever seemed more practical. Step two was to lure him or carry him to the basement, or some other place where Ma, her husband, and her vile offspring could have some privacy for step number three, which was simply to bash him in the head with an ax.

Ma went through the miner's pockets, and then his remains were stuffed in a canvas bag, all the shroud he was going to get. Once the body was rifled and bagged, what to do with it? The multitude of abandoned mine shafts in the area were the easy answer: just dump the remains down the hole. With something like three hundred shafts to choose from, and such a huge, transient population, who would know or care that another one of them went away someplace? In the unlikely case of somebody missing the victim, the body still would be lost, not only because of the number of shafts to choose from, but because so many were flooded.

For a while Ma's dirty scheme was both safe and profitable, and it might have gone on that way indefinitely, save for a harlot named Cora, long employed at Ma's house of joy. Cora knew quite a lot about the foul doings at Ma's place, and when Ma threw her out of the house, Cora acted. When she went knocking at the sheriff's door, the fat was in the fire for Ma and her clan.

Cora knew the names of some missing miners, who, she said, were last seen at Ma's and never again thereafter. Since a lot of miners had gone missing of late, and apparently Cora was persuasive, Ma and her husband and sons ended up in jail while a search went on for the remains. It was not easy, but the searchers stayed with it, even draining some of the shafts, and at last persistence paid off.

Floating in one of the shafts only two blocks from Main Street, a passer-by found the remains of a missing miner (sometimes called a "peddler") named Frank Galbraith, and that, along with Cora's testimony, was all that the prosecutor needed. Galbraith, according to the Galena Post, had been "shot through the head and body, throat cut" and robbed of some small amount.

There was more. A corn knife thought to be the weapon of the *coup de grace* was found in Ma's bed, of all places, adding more weight to the evidence. And the *Columbus Advocate* told of the attempted flight of George Staffleback, who fled from a constable at what the newspaper called "a Nancy Hanks gait," halting only when the officer leveled his pistol at him. As the paper put it, rather than hear the "dog bark," George gave it up, "telling the officer that he only wanted a little exercise." George did himself no good by running, since the whole world, including juries, tends to believe the biblical adjuration that "the wicked flee when no man pursueth."

There is an equally ugly alternative story. In this one, Galbraith was your typical town drunk, harmless, cheerful, spifflicated most of the time. And so he was on the evening of June 19, 1897, when he called on Ma's place to see a whore to whom he was especially attached and was rebuffed by old Ma Stafflebach. When Galbraith persisted, he was pursued through the street by her sons, until he finally fell and was knifed to death by Ed Stafflebach. His remains ended up in one of the omnipresent water-filled shafts—all but his hat, which Ma's "spouse" kept and cleaned up with soap and water.

Galbraith, badly decomposed, was found and identified by letters he was carrying in his pocket. The cause of death was abundantly clear, since he had been shot twice and his throat cut. It was not hard to decide who the killers were; two of Ma's girls talked freely, and the arrests followed—George Stafflebach was already in jail for another offense.

The family's reputation went before them. The News of Joplin, where the family had lived before, pulled no punches: "The Stafflebach family has been a disgrace to the human race in general and the inhabitants of Joplin and vicinity in particular for many years." Meanwhile, a second paper reported, "The Stafflebach gang formerly resided in this city, and much deviltry is charged up against them during their residence here."

The local press was not kind to the defendants either, as witness the Evening Times' comment on George Stafflebach's wife, also named Cora, that she "is George's wife, though he is in jail so much she never had a chance to live with him." Cora fared no better: "Cora is a very ignorant, coarse girl." The paper had some choice comments for the other defendants as well, advising the public that brother George was already in one jail, brother Mike was in another, and daddy had just gotten out of the slammer. Ma got hers, too: "The old lady is a perfect picture of an old hag or witch, the kind you've read about. She must be 60 or 65 years old."

Ma, her husband, and her sons were all convicted of complicity in Galbraith's murder and went off to prison, Ma as an accomplice to murder. She did twelve years of her twenty-one-year sentence before she died in 1909. To the last, she continued to protest her innocence.

Two of her sons got life sentences, her husband twenty-five years, and a third son, convicted of larceny, went up for seven years.

Only two more bodies of missing miners were ever found, though more searching went on. Considering the number of water-filled shafts available as burying sites, that is not surprising. Nor did any of Ma's estimated $50,000 in loot ever show up, even though her own house was disassembled nail by nail.

It is distinctly possible that Ma's loot is still out there somewhere, probably buried, and so, almost surely, are the bodies of dozens more missing men and two young harlots, who had joined the staff of the bordello the year before and were not seen again. Estimates of the number of Ma's victims run as high as fifty. Nobody will ever know the total.

Inevitably, there are tales of restless spirits haunting the old whorehouse. One news story billed the "Steffleback Bordello" as "a popular stop for area ghost hunters who savor the building's 'unwelcoming' ambience and who say the building is a hot spot for weird noises and other paranormal activity." Maybe so, considering the number of lives snuffed out by Ma and her boys.

Just as surely there were comparisons between Ma and another illustrious family of Kansas killers, the Bender clan (chapter 3). And indeed, accounts of Ma's modus operandi sound a little like those of the Benders, with the addition of the compliant harlots. The idea was for one of the girls to distract the victim, while one of Ma's boys sneaked up behind the victim and bashed him in the head through a curtain hung behind the sofa.

As late as the summer of 2012 a civic group was trying to raise the money needed to repair what is locally called the Steffleback Bordello; it is surely a part of Galena's history, and should not be lost. Not all history is beautiful.

CHAPTER FOURTEEN

Shady Ladies and Disreputable Damsels

The American westward movement was a wonderful thing: the vast, vigorous, hope-filled settlement of a whole continent, the expansion of a young, strong people who could not be stopped by war, outlawry, or the rigors of an unsympathetic mother nature. Had Americans not been the tough, eager, courageous folk they were, the boundaries of this young nation would have stopped at the Mississippi.

But there were troubles along the way: vicious winter weather; tough, hostile Indians fighting for their ancestral ground; violent outlaws by the dozen; swindlers and conmen; sickness; and above all, distance. It was simply an enormous long way to get to anywhere in a country without roads, crossed by mountain chains and broad rivers.

And there was seldom enough of anything: doctors and veterinarians and pastors pushed west with the immigrant stream, and if you were lucky one settled somewhere close to you—within twenty miles or so, that is. Often, especially in the early days, there wasn't even a nearby trading post or rudimentary little store where a family could buy staples.

There was another want most keenly felt by the single men pushing west: women. Booze there was; you could make that locally, even if some rotgut was bad enough to gag a maggot. But the fair sex was in terribly short supply, and the wives and daughters of west-bound families were off limits. Even an attempt to seduce one of these ladies was likely to get you killed by a father or a brother or some combination of these.

So man's most basic need was filled by the "ladies of the line," harlots who braved the way west to ply their ancient profession. Some of the pure-in-heart tended to look down their noses at these women, and lumped them together with the actual outlaw women; generally, in fact,

Cattle Annie and Little Britches

old-fashioned harlotry was not a crime, and the girls were at least tacitly understood to fill an important need.

And so the brothel became a fixture on the frontier. Depending on the growing gentility of their surroundings, the houses tended to be more or less silent partners of a settlement's life. They were there, of course, and everybody in town knew it, but you didn't talk much about such things in polite society. Sometimes, of course, the rougher towns boasted notable exceptions, like this one: "Madame Lucy: Ye Old Whore Shoppe." but such blatant advertising was not done in more civilized settlements.

The girls tended to acquire nicknames, too. For example, there were Rotary Rosie—I'd like to know how she came by that name—Slanting Annie, Velvet Ass Rose, Sallie Purple, and Madame Featherlegs. The names were catchy, and in the frontier prostitution business, it paid to advertise.

Most of the brothels of course offered whiskey and many also put on non-carnal entertainment. The entertainers—many of them singers who couldn't sing on key and dancers who couldn't dance to speak of— rivaled the harlots in the exotic name contest: the Galloping Cow, her dancing partner the Dancing Heifer, the Waddling Duck, the Little Lost Chicken, and so on. Often, these ladies doubled in brass as soiled doves. Often they didn't rate very high in either the pulchritude sweepstakes or the talent contest—but boy, were they entertaining, particularly after a half-dozen shots of premium snake oil.

And the ladies of the evening kept things interesting in more than their professional capacity. Take the madam who ran a house at a woebegone place called Beer City, out in the dusty Oklahoma panhandle. She rejoiced in the felicitous name of Pussycat Nell and she was a strong-minded woman, not the kind who put up tamely with thugs and bullies.

Nell managed to get crosswise with the local "sheriff," an apparently self-appointed lawman who exploited the local tradesmen by "protecting" them and their businesses and charging as his fee for this benevolence whatever they had that he wanted. Pussycat resented his high-handed ways, and when he got around to exacting his law enforcement fee from her—presumably in her girls' services—she simply took a shotgun to him; exit the "sheriff."

There is no record that Nell was ever prosecuted for the killing, or that anybody even considered it, perhaps because the good sheriff was widely known do some rustling as a sidelight. His departure from this Earth seems to have been another example of western justice under the headings of "he had it coming," coupled with "who cares?"

Others of the shady lady sorority were less than serious members of the outlaw community. Little Britches and Cattle Annie, who orbited around the notorious Doolin gang, were proclaimed as outlaws by some writers, aptly classified as only "groupies" by others. Born Jennie Stevenson and Anna McDoulet, they were farmed out as youngsters to be other people's domestic servants. It didn't take the two long to decide that the never-ending, unglamorous, backbreaking work that was the lot of an ill-paid servant girl was not for them.

Both of the girls seem to have become precocious sexual athletes: Little Britches, for instance, had been married twice by the time she was sixteen, at which age she met Cattle Annie. Both of them gravitated toward outlaws of the Doolin bunch and dressed the part, male garb, saddle horses, pistol belts and all. They struck out on their own, too, doing a little rustling and considerable bootlegging, and at the same time running a sort of on-call information service for Doolin.

There was a certain attraction, a kind of special panache that characterized some of the West's most famous outlaws. For one thing, they were somebody, different, somehow romantic, who defied authority, who dared to take chances and do things that others did not. That attraction touched women sometimes, not just schoolgirls mooning over a daring outlaw they heard about, say, a youngster called Jesse James. There was more to it than that. Sometimes it was enough to draw an otherwise normal girl away from family and friends into the chilly, dark world of the outlaw.

On the surface, the outlaw world could look exciting, far more entrancing than having swarms of children, trying to keep a rickety house clean, and maybe following the south end of a mule down endless furrows during plowing time.

So it was with two otherwise ordinary girls from southwest Missouri, Jennie Stevenson and Anna Emmaline McDoulet. Both girls loved the purple prose of the most successful dime novelist of all time, Ned

Buntline. Among other topics on which Buntline ground out breathtaking tales was the gang headed by Bill Doolin, and in the fullness of time the two girls managed to join that ill-fated bunch down in northeast Indian Territory, as Oklahoma was then. Or not, for according to another account neither girl became part of Doolin's gang.

Whether they ran with Doolin or not, they quickly became a thorn in the side of the law, selling whiskey to the Indian tribes and stealing other people's stock. They remained outlaw "groupies" too, alerting wanted men of pursuers wearing stars. They of course had to adopt swashbuckling names, just like the big boys did, and so Jennie became Little Britches and Anna was called Cattle Annie. They were still in their early teens.

It didn't last. Finally—or so the story goes—after exchanging fire with tough lawman Bill Tilghman they were run down and passed into captivity. In 1895 Annie got a year and Little Britches two for bootlegging to the Indians and rustling; Little Britches' extra year was apparently a reward for shooting at the law men who came to arrest her. It was a light sentence, the girls would soon be out of prison, and they had arrived, or so it must have seemed to these outlaw wannabes.

Unfortunately for the two girls, once they were gone up the river they ceased to be news. There are all sorts of stories about their later days, but the most likely are these: once released, Little Britches got lucky—she married, had children, and became part of the society she had once abandoned. Cattle Annie was not so lucky: free, she had to find work, and ended up as a . . . domestic servant. Already ill with tuberculosis, she was dead within a year or two.

The women who really built the new land were not nearly as colorful as these two. But they did the hard work: They made homes, raised families under the worst possible conditions, bore many children and sometimes died in the process, worked long, long hours beside their husbands in blistering sun and icy rain, buried children and parents, and still found time to help establish churches and schools and bring a touch of grace into a hostile land.

The books and films are mostly about the women with colorful nicknames and sinful habits, as is this book. It is good to remember while we enjoy their deeds and legends, that it was their quiet, honest sisters who really built the United States.

CHAPTER FIFTEEN

Lady Macbeth

Kathryn Kelly

Ace Atkins, Pulitzer Prize–winning novelist, called Kathryn Kelly "The Lady Macbeth of America," and the title is right on the money. Although we're not positive she murdered anybody, she did enough other ugly stuff that at the least she deserves the title of Ms. Public Enemy.

The practice of officially nominating criminals as "public enemies" and numbering them, presumably in order of importance, probably had no discernible impact on the crime rate in the America of the 1920s and 1930s, but it sure was entertaining. You could bet on who would be next week's Public Enemy Number One, and there was lots of competition for that dubious honor. Most of the big newspaper names in the world of crime made the list from time to time.

One of these was a genial Irishman named George Kelly, to be ever-after known as "Machinegun Kelly." Kelly was tough enough in fact, but he grew bigger and scarier with time, manipulated like a puppet, so the story goes, not only by the press but by his lover.

That lover is one of the more interesting women in the history of crime. She started simply enough in life, born plain old Cleo Coleman down in Saltillo, Mississippi. Like a lot of the ladies that went on to be major-league molls, she got a running start toward stardom, married a laborer named Fry before she was sixteen, had a daughter, and then ceased being Mrs. Fry in short order. She advanced to running bootleg hooch for, of all people, her mother, and along the way married—briefly—one Allie Brewer.

"Machine Gun" Kelly and wife received life sentences for Urschel kidnapping

She discarded him and got married again when she was twenty to local bootlegger Charlie Thorne. That marriage ended in 1927 when Charlie committed suicide, or so the coroner decided. There has long been a lingering question of whether Charlie's abrupt exodus from life was somehow helped along. If it was, some have asked whether Cleo, by now using the more cultivated name Kathryn—note the spiffy spelling—might somehow have assisted in his departure.

There is a story that she shot Thorne herself and left an appropriately pitiful note. He is supposed to have written, "I cannot live with her or without her, hence, I am departing this life." There is no record of any such note, nor any clue that suggests he wrote one. One source even says he was illiterate. Maybe the note was some reporter's invention. All the same, the aura of "black widow" that would follow Kathryn in later years got its start with the letter that nobody ever saw.

And with one other story: there is a tale that Kathryn, away from home in Coleman, Texas, and hearing that Thorne was cheating on her, drove off for home. She is said to have stopped for gas along the way and announced to the station attendant, "I'm bound for Coleman, Texas, to kill that god dammed Charlie Thorne." The story is way too pat to be believable, but stranger things have happened.

Anyway, whether Charlie passed to his reward entirely on his own or had some help, he ended up dead the next day.

The next several years Kathryn spent bouncing around Texas and Oklahoma. She was not idle, having been busted along the way for prostitution, robbery, and shoplifting. All of this was apparently in addition to her basic trade of bootlegging, which was also her mother's profession, and her cousin's. Crime was a sort of family affair, so perhaps it came naturally. Her aunt was a hooker, and she had a couple of uncles in the slammer, one for counterfeiting, the other for auto theft.

She was good at things illegal and sufficiently frugal that she saved enough money to live high on the hog. One boyfriend, who caught her between husbands, had this comment to make about the high-living Kathryn, how she took him to "more speakeasies, bootleg dives, and holes in the wall, than I thought there were in all of Texas. She knows more bums than the police department. She can drink liquor like water. And she's got some of the toughest friends I ever laid eyes on."

All of which made it natural, or at least easier, for Kathryn to turn to bigger things in the world of crime. After all, she was working as a manicurist, which did not quite permit the sort of broad horizons that appealed to her. And in the late 1920s, she met Kelly—the great meeting is said to have occurred in Leavenworth Prison, where he was an inmate, she being there to call on her uncles. Somewhere around this time she became the mistress of a hood called Little Steve Anderson in Oklahoma City, and when Kelly got out of prison he went to work for Anderson.

Now Kelly, born George Francis Barnes Jr., had been a small-time bootlegger himself, and along the way he had adopted the name Kelly to help cover his tracks. He didn't cover them well enough to avoid a federal arrest for running bootleg hooch onto an Indian reservation. That got him three years in Leavenworth and a start on a new career.

There's another story that Kathryn met Kelly in Fort Worth in 1928 or before. In this version, they met in a honky-tonk in Fort Worth, or at least Kelly said they did. "She was pretty, the prettiest redhead I ever saw."

No matter how and where romance between Kelly and Kathryn blossomed, once it did the pair ran off together, taking, it is said, both Anderson's car and, of all things, his bulldog. They ended up in Minneapolis, got married, and looked about for new worlds to conquer. Certainly Kathryn did, if you believe the story that, by golly, she was going to turn Kelly into a world-beater of a criminal.

Part one of this saga is the tale of the Thompson submachinegun, the weapon that turned Kelly into Machinegun Kelly (not to be confused with Machinegun Jack McGurn, another famous name of the time). Now, part of the Machinegun Kelly myth was that he was a hero of World War I, in which he used his trusty tommy gun to help carry the fight to the Kaiser.

Another part of the Kelly myth is that Kathryn bought Kelly his first Thompson at a Fort Worth pawn shop, and made him practice with it until he was so proficient he could write his name with the weapon and shoot walnuts off a fence at an amazing twenty-five paces—which sounds marvelous, except that anybody who has fired a Thompson will tell you that the weapon, fired automatically, climbs so strongly that knocking batches of nuts off a fence would have be considered miraculous; after the first nut, all bets are off.

Kelly might well have used the Thompson in combat, except that he missed the war, having been medically deferred from the draft. Even had he served, there was another minor difficulty: the Thompson gun did not make its appearance on active service until 1919. Still and all, he at least found out how to use one post-war, and, thanks in part to Kathryn's hype, achieved a sort of renown in the criminal world—and the newspapers—as Machinegun George Kelly. Kathryn referred to Kelly as "the big guy," and even handed out tommy gun cartridges as a sort of calling-card souvenir.

Kelly's criminal career ranged over various episodes of armed robbery—including a $70,000 bank heist—but the big one that every criminal dreams about was still to come. They had tried a kidnapping in South Bend, Indiana, but released their captive after he gave them a promissory note, which of course turned out to be worthless. Allegedly, repeated demands for payment over the next several months went unanswered.

But, if at first you don't succeed . . . and so they tried again, with much improved results. The kidnapping of Charles Urschel of Oklahoma City should have been the big bonanza, for Urschel came of a wealthy family, their assets including a thriving brewery. The Kellys got their ransom, all right, but they had also bought into a world of trouble; they had snatched the wrong man.

For Urschel was not only intelligent, but he had a world of guts. Blindfolded he knew not where, he memorized sounds, counted footsteps over distances that might be important, even listened to aircraft passing overhead and intentionally left fingerprints everywhere he could reach. He remembered the bitter-tasting water and his captors' talk about their robberies, even their deprecating chatter about Bonnie and Clyde. His determination and photographic memory would pay big dividends.

Kathryn Kelly showed her true colors during the long debate about what to do with their hostage. Mother Ora and her stepfather probably heard a significant part of this, as their lovely daughter argued—in the hearing of the blindfolded Urschel—for his murder. She is quoted as saying, "What I think is that we're a bunch of saps if we turn this son-of-a-bitch loose! Kill the bastard! Then we won't have any more trouble with him."

But Kelly and his sidekick Albert Bates wanted no part of this unladylike suggestion, and Kathryn was overruled.

Once the ransom was paid—a monumental and record $200,000—
and Urschel released, the Kellys could have made tracks to enjoy their pile
of money, but Urschel's keen memory made that impossible. So did the
Kellys' bone-headed refusal to drive away, fast and far. Urschel, carrying
his own shotgun, even joined the police raid on the confederates' farm
where he'd been held.

The Kellys did have a little time to enjoy their coup. In St. Paul, then
a mecca for big-time outlaws, folks like Dillinger and the Barkers and
the like, they turned their hot money into cooler bills—at a more than 50
percent bite—and indulged. Kelly, it is said, got a brand-new Thompson
and a case of whiskey, and his bride bought herself a 16-cylinder auto-
mobile, a thousand-dollar ring, a platinum watch studded with more than
two hundred diamonds, and a huge and expensive wardrobe—and this in
1933 dollars.

They didn't have time to really enjoy all that luxury. For inexplicable
reasons they went to ground in a Memphis boardinghouse, quarreling
over their next move but doing nothing. Kathryn took to ridiculing her
husband, calling him "Pop-Gun Kelly," and in the end he had finally had
enough. This, if the quote is accurate, is what he said to her later when
the grand passion was cooling: "I was the biggest damn fool in the world
to ever let you suck me into this thing. Here I was, making a grand a year
knocking over those tin-can state banks, but that wasn't good enough.
Now we've got heat smeared all over us. And you got me into this mess."

Which wasn't strictly true, Kelly being of age to say no, but Kelly had
never demonstrated either strength of character or much in the way of
intelligence in the past. He failed again to show either.

The raiders ran down Kelly, who was arrested without resistance one
early morning by officers of the Memphis police. "I've been waiting for
you," he said to the arresting officers. Kelly had his pockets full of ransom
money, which made the appearance of innocence even less convincing.
And here another small American legend got its genesis.

As the raiders crashed in, Kelly is supposed to have yelled, "Don't
shoot, G-men; don't shoot, G-men!" although he almost surely didn't; the
term, supposedly short for "government men" as far as anybody knows,
had not been heard before. It became popular in a hurry afterward.

And in any case, it does not appear that the FBI was involved in the arrest at all. Stories about the bureau's participation, according to at least one source, were simply part of the mythology cranked out by J. Edgar Hoover. Kathryn tried to trade her lover's freedom for that of her harridan mother, Ora, already in jail, and a light sentence for herself. So much for true love. That didn't work, and so she tried letters to prosecutors threatening the Urschel family, and one to Urschel himself suggesting that if the Kellys' confederates in the kidnapping were not released, "you can get another rich wife in hell."

Once she was arrested, she staged a phony appendicitis attack and gave a newspaper interview in which she said she wouldn't have become involved in all this if Kelly hadn't threatened her. She did the same thing during their kidnapping trial. "The Big Guy" was no longer her star.

The Kellys, tried for kidnapping, got the book thrown at them: The sentence was life in prison, in this, the first federal prosecution under the newly minted Lindbergh Law, the only good consequence of the tragic kidnapping and death of the aviation hero's baby. Kathryn's mother, Ora, got the same sentence. More than $73,000 in ransom money was recovered from a Texas cotton patch. Much of the rest is still missing.

Kelly would not see the outside of prison again. He finished his life inside, bragging about all the tough, wonderful things he'd done, nicknamed by the cons, according to one story, "Pop-gun" Kelly, the same endearing name coined by Kathryn.

Kathryn, on the other hand, made it all the way through to 1985, dying quietly, unheralded, in Tulsa. She had been released, along with Mama Ora, in 1958, the same year that rising star Charles Bronson played Machinegun Kelly on the silver screen. Her release was based in part on an allegation that the prosecution had suppressed evidence that Kathryn was not the author of the Urschel ransom letters.

Both she and Ora both went to work in a home for the elderly and when she was interviewed four years later Kathryn again blamed poor old George for everything: "I was just a young farm girl when I met George back in 1930. I wasn't used to all the money, cars, and jewelry George offered me . . . any farm girl would have been swept off her feet same as I was." She departed this earth from a Tulsa nursing home. Mother Ora had beaten her to the Pearly Gates—or wherever she went—four years before.

And lest there be any doubt that good triumphs over evil in the end, there is the tale of Kathryn's daughter Pauline. It is said that Pauline was able to go to college courtesy of an anonymous donor—none other than Charles Urschel, ably assisted by a judge who'd also been showered with death threats by the Kellys.

The good guys won that one.

CHAPTER SIXTEEN

Death Wore a Veil

Henrietta Robinson

Today, Henrietta Robinson—if that was really her name—would probably have ended up in a psychiatric hospital before she did anything really
seriously criminal; she certainly had obvious mental problems, not least
of which was a consuming paranoia. But back in the middle of the nineteenth century the answers to question of mental capacity were not nearly
as clear as they appear to be these days.

That was back before Freud, Jung, and Adler had galloped onto
the psychiatric scene, before anybody talked much about the Theory of
Dreams or had any real ideas of what psychoses were and what they were
supposed to do to people. And you have to suspect that in those days
those who enforced the law were less concerned with criminals' mental
acuity than their modern counterparts must be.

Henrietta's case was a perplexing thing from beginning to end. To
start with, nobody was ever sure what her name really was. And then there
were the black veils she perpetually wore; for although she was a beautiful woman, and a well-known citizen of Troy, New York, at mid-century,
people also knew that Henrietta was not her real name and it was hard to
say what she really looked like.

What they did know for a certainty was that she was paranoid, suspicious of everybody, to the point that if anybody said anything to her that
might be construed as an insult, she pulled her revolver and demanded an
apology. She was convinced that she faced a widespread conspiracy.

And that was not her only peculiarity. Even her background was a
mystery, for she told several different stories about it. In one she was the

daughter of a lord, driven from the family castle by her father. In another she was persecuted by an evil stepmother. In still another, she was convinced that a neighbor—also a conspirator—had somehow halted navigation on the Hudson River.

She had been found wandering about in the dark through public buildings asking for the police, convinced that her home was in danger from this faceless conspiracy, and demanding protection. Anybody who seemed curious about her odd behavior ran the risk of looking down the muzzle of her revolver.

She lived in a cottage with an elderly gardener and a servant girl, but she did not stay there often enough to please her neighbors, for Henrietta was much given to wandering the streets of Troy at night, always carrying her revolver. On at least one occasion she left home at night wearing only a nightgown and woke up a friend to ask for the loan of a dress. "I guess I forgot to dress when I left home," she said. Sure enough, Henrietta was distinctly not the girl next door.

Now close to Henrietta's cottage was a little store, run by a couple name Lanagan who lived in rooms attached to the store. From time to time Henrietta would send the servant girl over to the store for provisions, including prodigious amounts of beer and brandy. Sometimes she would go in herself to drink with other *habitués*, but she always seemed to bring with her both her suspicious disposition and her revolver. More than once she got herself ejected from the Lanagans' pub. She was not a popular neighbor.

And then on a day in May, she got into an argument with another patron at Lanagan's, and things became so heated that at last Mrs. Lanagan asked her to leave. She did, but later returned while the Lanagans were having dinner with Catharine Lubee, their sister or sister-in-law. The Lanagans invited Henrietta to eat with them, which she did. After the meal she offered to buy more beer for everybody. Miss Lubee and Mr. Lanagan accepted. Mrs. Lanagan declined, and that little word "no" saved her life.

For sweet Henrietta provided the beer all right, but she also loaded it with arsenic. She had also laced the beer with sugar, a treat for the taste, she said, but then she left the store. Mr. Lanagan and Miss Lubee tried

Henrietta Robinson

this odd concoction, covered with sugar yet oddly bitter, and before the night was out both became deathly ill. And deathly it turned out to be.

There was no doubt about what killed them; their bodies were full of arsenic. Nor was there any question about who provided it. The prosecution located the druggist who sold Henrietta the poison, discovered more arsenic in Henrietta's cottage, and had the compelling testimony of Mrs. Lanagan about the odd sugary beer with the bitter aftertaste.

Henrietta had even gone to the druggist just before her arrest to remind him that she had bought the arsenic "to kill rodents." She also said she needed help, and because she had refused to lend the Lanagans money, she was being accused out of revenge. And then she went back to an old paranoiac theme: "[t]he entire neighborhood is against me, and I think they mean to do me harm."

The druggist said she might get help from the chief of police, who rejoiced in the appropriate name of Amasa Copp. She did not have to see him, for she was soon arrested by Chief Copp's minions. In jail she seemed to live in a world of her own; a doctor who saw her repeatedly said, "On all occasions, I was satisfied that she was not a rational woman."

So were many people who watched her at trial. She dressed entirely in black, including the black veils—five layers of them—which made her so famous. Her clothing was immaculate, right down to her spotless white gloves, a life-sized figurine with a voice but no face.

Henrietta had been quickly arrested, but the indictment process seemed to take forever, to the point that some people supposed she was being protected by someone powerful. While she was in jail awaiting trial she added to the mystery by drinking vitriol—acid—by mistake, an error some concluded was evidence of "powerful forces" trying to silence her.

But at length the case ground on to trial and there was enough excitement to satisfy the most avid scandal-monger. Said one paper, she was the daughter of a Montreal doctor who had died some years before in an asylum. Given her peculiarities, that seemed a reasonable possibility. Another paper identified her as a bar owner who had eloped with a cabbie, and still a third said no, she was really the daughter of an Irish gentleman of high social rank; she had married her father's steward and been driven from the family hearth in disgrace as a result.

This was the sort of stuff the public loved so well (still does), and there was even more to come—and that juicier. A woman identified her as a classmate at the Troy Female Seminary, a woman named Wood. That provoked a quick and angry response from the Wood family. No, they said, a thousand times no, she is not one of ours.

The trial produced sensational news almost from the beginning. There was the matter of the black veil, for one thing. About three days into the trial, the judge told her to take it off. No, she said, go right ahead and hold me in contempt. I won't take it off for anybody, said Henrietta, and she made it stick, even over the advice of her lawyer. And on one occasion the druggist who sold her the arsenic caught a glimpse beneath the veil and, according to one story, "fell back in horror. Henrietta had been smiling at him, a hideous, maniacal smile full of gleaming teeth."

Nor could anybody establish anything certain about her but more and more of the wild tales Henrietta had told of herself. They ranged from the story that her husband was a "great lord in Ireland" to her ability to swim until she was tired and then rest while she supported herself on a cork clutched between her teeth. She had grown up, she said variously, in a French chateau and an English nunnery. And on and on.

But the jury had a different view of her distinct peculiarities, whatever the papers might say, regardless of the evidence they heard. The jurors seemed to take the view that acting like an ass and telling wild tales of oneself is not the same thing as being truly crazy, and the verdict was guilty of murder in the first degree. Henrietta kept up her act even after the verdict. "Shame on you, judge," she yelled, "shame on you! There is corruption here; there is corruption here!"

There surely was, but it was all Henrietta's.

On sentence day, she relented enough raise her veil, just in time to hear the sentence of death by hanging. The appellate process dragged on and on after that, and by the time it was finished enough people had petitioned the governor asking for clemency that her sentence was commuted to life in prison. She never came out of Sing Sing until at last she was transferred to a psychiatric facility. She died there, and, according to legend, nobody ever knew her real name.

CHAPTER SEVENTEEN

A Message from Hell

Lavinia Fisher

Back in the first decade of the nineteenth century, Lavinia Fisher and her husband were innkeepers, landlords of Six Mile House, an inn outside Charleston, South Carolina. It was an inviting place, well kept and comfortable, and the lovely Lavinia was a marvelous hostess. The bloody Benders and the evil Ma Staffleback were still to come in the annals of hostel crime, so there was nothing to which to compare lonely Six Mile House and its genial proprietors. Yet. But there were unsettling rumors that some travelers who checked into Six Mile House seemed never to have checked out again.

Take the case of John Peoples. Peoples was a fur trader who stopped one night at Six Mile House and was almost overwhelmed by the Fishers' hospitality. They were, he thought, far too friendly, especially the lovely Lavinia, and it made him so uncomfortable that he went to bed early.

He remained uncomfortable, and for good reason. Restless and apprehensive, he passed up the bed and sat down in a chair where he could watch the door. It was as well that he did. For deep in the night the bed dropped through a trapdoor into the cellar. Down below stood Fisher with an axe. Peoples wisely decided he'd seen enough and hurried from the inn; he hied himself straight to Charleston and the police.

The authorities discovered a lime pit in the cellar, not the usual equipment for a country inn. Worse, in that pit were a couple of bodies. Once the wheels of justice got to turning, John Fisher tried to blame all this evil doing on Lavinia, but it didn't do him a bit of good. They hung together—Lavinia all duded up in her wedding dress—or at least that's the traditional story of the evil proprietors of Six Mile House.

There's another version. Along about the time this tale begins, the countryside around Charleston was infested with highwaymen, who seemed to operate on the highway in the area around two buildings: Six Mile House and Five Mile House. All the police had were lots of suspicions and lots of angry businessmen, for the drayage trade had an important effect on the economy of Charleston.

And so a band of local citizens decided to act on their own. Since the rules of evidence meant nothing to them, they had far greater freedom to act than the public servants of Charleston. The Charleston *News and Courier* put it pretty well:

> *A gang of desperadoes have for some time past occupied certain houses . . . frequently committing robberies upon defenseless travelers. As they could not be identified . . . it was determined, by a number of citizens, to break them up and they . . . proceeded in a cavalcade . . . to the spot . . . having previously obtained permission of the owners of some small houses, to which these desperadoes resorted, to proceed against the premises in such manner as circumstances might require.*

Five Mile House was the first stop. The vigilantes gave everybody in the structure a quarter of an hour to go someplace else, and then burned the building down. Six Mile House was next, but here the law-and-order boys simply threw everybody out and left a guard to prevent outlaw reoccupation. The guard, a man named Ross, found the job more than one man could handle, for the outlaws returned in force. He was driven outside, where he was surrounded by about a dozen of them, all men—and one woman: Lavinia. He asked her for help, but all he got was a choking and his head shoved through a window.

In the midst of all this, John Peoples innocently stopped to water his horse. The mob surrounded him, too, and relieved him of about $40, a substantial sum in those far-off days. Peoples headed straight for Charleston. He couldn't identify all of the highwaymen, but he did know two of them, Roberts and Andrews, and he knew the lone woman, Lavinia Fisher.

So nemesis descended on the area of Six Mile House, and John and Lavinia were swept into the bag along with several others and carted off to jail. While they awaited trial for highway robbery, a couple of bodies turned up buried near Six Mile House. They were thought to be the remains of a black woman and a white man, buried at least two years before. They were the only bodies found, contrary to myth, far from the Bender-style charnel house of mythology.

But, highway robbery carried the death penalty in those days, whether the victim lost his life or not, and that is what the Fishers got—both of them. While the case was up on appeal, they were kept in the debtors' prison area of the Charleston lockup. Security was not as tight there as it was in regular jails, and the two managed to drive a hole through the wall beneath a window. John went out first, but the rope of blankets broke under his weight, leaving Lavinia in the cell. Oddly, quixotically, John elected to not to go on with his escape, but to stay with his wife.

When the appeal failed, there was nothing left but the hanging. A clergyman came to their cell to give such spiritual comfort as he could. He "made some headway with John, but Lavinia was more likely to curse than pray." She sure did some swearing on hanging day, when she "stamped in rage and swore with all the vehemence of her amazing vocabulary, calling down damnation on a governor who would let a woman swing. . . . she . . . ended with a volley of shrieks."

John Fisher took a moment on the scaffold to express his contrition, and a letter was read in which he thanked the clergyman for spiritual enlightenment, but Lavinia wasn't having any of that. Her last words typed this lovely lady for all time: "If you have a message you want to send to hell give it to me. I'll carry it."

Maybe she did.

CHAPTER EIGHTEEN

"You Can't Chop Your Momma Up in Massachusetts"

Lizzie Borden

"You can't chop your momma up in Massachusetts, not even if you're tired of her cuisine." So sang the Chad Mitchell trio, and it was so. You couldn't chop your poppa up either, but that happened as well, and a well-bred, apparently Christian young woman named Elizabeth accomplished both these feats in quick succession. It happened in the quiet, conservative, not to say stodgy, town of Fall River back in the summer of 1892.

The double killing was a considerable sensation for the time. After all, one just didn't *do* that sort of thing in Fall River, especially in good families. It even inspired a kids' rhyme, thus:

> Elizabeth Borden took an axe,
> and gave her father forty whacks;
> and when the job was neatly done,
> she gave her mother forty-one.

Or maybe she didn't, as some later writers and arm-chair sleuths have speculated.

Andrew Borden was a prosperous businessman, well known in Fall River. On this day, much like any other, he had gone to run sundry errands, and when he returned home had apparently felt the need of a nap, or at least a brief rest. He sat down on a couch downstairs in the sitting room and somebody came along and chopped him into barely recognizable chunks with a hatchet. His daughter Elizabeth, as she told it, found him dead, and called frantically to the Borden maid, Bridget, then in her upstairs room.

The family doctor was called, neighbors hurried over to care for Lizzie, and while they were tending to her, Bridget went upstairs and found Abby Borden, Lizzie's stepmother, lying on the floor of her bedroom, also hacked virtually beyond recognition. Somebody had knocked her down, then sat on her and whopped her in the back of the head a dozen times or more.

The police jumped to the obvious conclusion: nobody was home at the Borden house but Lizzie and Bridget; ergo, it was highly likely that one of them was the killer. On the strength of what was called contradictory and confused inquest testimony, Lizzie was arrested a couple of days later.

Now, all was not sweetness and light in the Borden household, even if this was Massachusetts. Lizzie and her elder sister, Emma—who was not at home the day of the murders—had become estranged from their parents, to the point that they no longer ate together. Lizzie even called her stepmother "Mrs. Borden." The problem, or at least a part of it, was that Borden *père* was giving away a summer home that the girls thought should rightfully be theirs.

Both sisters had taken what has been called an "extended vacation," returning home only about a week before the murders. Lizzie stayed away four more days, staying in a local rooming house before coming home.

—◦—

While being questioned by the police, Lizzie had run off at the mouth, contradicting herself and managing to look guilty as sin. She said at various times that she had been in three different places in the house when her father came home, and that she had put his slippers on him—in the face of police photos showing him still wearing his boots. And at the inquest she refused to answer some questions even though the answers could have helped her.

Since the inquest was "private" by statute, she had no counsel present to protect her, even though she had asked for one, and had been prescribed morphine to "calm her nerves." What affect that may have had on her understanding and perception is unknown.

But as every criminal lawyer knows, in any major felony prosecution, the devil is in the details. For one thing, there was the question of the blood. Hacking somebody into chunks releases a vast amount of blood, let alone chopping up two people one after another. The hacker would logically be soaked with gore, without, in Lizzie's case, time and opportunity to get herself and her clothing clean and dry in the very limited time before she "discovered" her father's body.

But Lizzie wasn't bloody.

There were other things, too. Bridget had heard nothing, seen nothing. There was a hatchet with a broken handle down in the cellar, but it showed no signs of blood, and experts testified that within the very limited timeframe there would not have been enough time to thoroughly clean it. There were other axe blades as well, but the same lack of blood disqualified them as well.

The case was a mass of contradictions. Lizzie denied being upstairs, although Bridget said she heard Lizzie's laughter up the stairs. Lizzie said she next went to the barn to find a piece of metal to repair a door, and then remained in the barn loft eating pears for twenty to thirty minutes. This the police doubted, because of the stifling heat in the loft. Then she gave another version, saying now that she had spent only ten minutes away from the house, this time looking for sinkers for her father's planned fishing trip. She returned to the house, in both versions, only to find her father dead.

At first she also said that she had heard a noise, perhaps a groan or call for help, before she entered the house. Then that changed too, when she said she had heard nothing before going back to the house.

With all Lizzie's confused explanations, the case against her was reasonably strong: motive and opportunity were both there, well supported by some lesser factors. For instance, an officer had seen Lizzie at night bending over the pails containing her parents' bloody clothing, and she had burned a dress in the stove, claiming it was paint-stained.

The police said they found her attitude unhelpful and uncongenial, for obvious reasons, but the jury was not persuaded beyond a reasonable doubt. The jury agreed there was too much uncertainty, and Lizzie walked free.

The elder Borden may have been a keen business man, but he was otherwise a skinflint. The house in Fall River not only was in a less-than-desirable part of town, but had no interior plumbing, not a thing to please the ladies. Sisters Lizzie and Emma now had a substantial inheritance available to them, part of which they invested

Lizzie Borden

in a much larger Fall River house, a place they named Maplecroft. There they lived in some luxury, surrounded by servants, until Emma moved out in 1905, allegedly after a quarrel with her sister.

Lizzie lasted until 1927, dying of pneumonia. Emma followed her just nine days later; she passed away in the nursing home to which she had gone in part to escape the public view, for the years between had seen Lizzie—Lisbeth as she now called herself—a social outcast in their little world of Fall River. The effect must have overflowed to deeply darken Emma's life as well. All the money in the world could not make up for years of suspicion and isolation.

So who chopped up Lizzie's parents? That mystery is beyond solving. There have been all sorts of theories floated over the years: Lizzie and Bridget were having a lesbian affair and her parents found out; Emma, moved by greed, established an alibi and then returned to do the deed; Bridget lashed out at her cruel employers; Lizzie did it after all.

Or, it could have been somebody else altogether. It is said that Father Borden was about as popular as the flu around Fall River, so it could have been somebody who detested him or got crossways with him on a business deal. That person could then have walked off, bloody clothing, bloody axe and all, without leaving a trace, although it's hard to theorize why Mrs. Borden should have been murdered too. Unless she surprised her husband's killer in the act or trying to leave the house.

There is no end to the books and articles written about Lizzie and the Fall River murders. There is also at least one movie, an opera, and even a ballet called "Fall River Suite," and perhaps best of all there is or was a Lizzie Borden Society, whose journal or newsletter is appropriately called *The Hatchet*.

So who done it?

We'll never know.

CHAPTER NINETEEN

The Empty Ones

The Dragon Lady and Shoebox Annie

The careers of these two women did not coincide, nor did they last long. The two were not friends; they were not related; they did not even know one another; they did not do their foul deeds in the same part of the United States. But one thing they did share: an emptiness inside, an awful emptiness; they looked like anybody else, but they weren't.

They had no soul.

Lydia Sherman, whom we shall call the Dragon Lady, was an attractive woman. She was a housewife and mother, but her only real concern in all the world was herself. She was the perfect friend and next-door neighbor—that is, until she saw something she wanted.

She was the wife of a New York policeman and the mother of six children, until the notion occurred to her to try a new and richer lifestyle. She started with a very small investment, only ten cents. That's all it cost her to buy some white arsenic from a druggist in the spring of 1864. The man who waited on her asked if she intended to kill rats, and Lydia told him, "Rats, my goodness, we're alive with rats!" Perhaps she was having a little private joke, because her intended victims were her own family.

It was not just a case of "I wanna be free," for she had made sure that everybody in the family was insured. Her husband was first. After she had watched him go in terrible pain, she could get to work on her six children.

Now that took time. Her children ranged in age from fourteen years to nine months and you couldn't very well poison them all at once; surely that would arouse suspicion. It would be hard enough making so many deaths look innocent over two years, which was the period Lydia chose.

She was a pretty fair actress, too, for she almost pulled it off. With floods of tears she managed to convince a series of doctors of the sincerity of her grief, and the deaths were chalked up to diverse fevers and epidemic diseases, even bronchitis.

Once she had cleared the inconvenience of the deaths of a whole family and collected her money, she moved her operations to New Haven, Connecticut in 1868. There she found her next victim, a rich farmer who also happened to be senile or getting there. She poisoned him as well and inherited his estate.

By the spring of 1870, Lydia was ready for further adventures. This time it was another prosperous man named Dennis Hurlbut, a widower, for whom she went to work as a housekeeper at his home in Derby, Connecticut. One thing led to another, and before long she was married again. Now Hurlbut had a little son, and he was the first to go, dead within hours of Lydia's tender ministrations. Next came Hurlbut's fourteen-year-old daughter. She got two cups of what was described as "very strong tea" in December of 1870 and was dead before the New Year.

By that time Hurlbut was turning into an alcoholic, grieving over the loss of his children, and he was easy, or at least he should have been. This time the quietus was a succession of cups of comforting chocolate; he was dead by the middle of May in 1871.

But here Lydia hit a snag. The doctors she had dealt with heretofore had fallen easy prey to her tears and practiced mask of sadness. This time the physician who had attended Hurlbut smelled a rat. He and two other doctors examined Hurlbut's body and those of the two children, and found all of them full of arsenic.

Lydia panicked and fled to New York, but the Connecticut police were right behind her. She stood trial as "The Queen Poisoner," so dubbed by the press, and curiously was convicted only of second-degree murder. Now if you deliberately poison people it is reasonable to conclude that you are necessarily demonstrating premeditation, so the verdict is a little hard to understand except perhaps as pursuant to a pretrial agreement.

She gave a long, rambling sort of confession, admitting eleven known murders, but the speculation was that she committed as many as ten or fifteen more. Those judicial admissions indicate a mind slipping away from reality, or maybe the requirements of a "deal" struck with the prosecution. Among other things that she said was an eerie explanation for killing her first husband: "I gave him the arsenic because I was discouraged. I know that that is not much of an excuse, but I felt so much trouble that I did not think about it."

In any case, the sentence was life. She died in 1878.

Which brings us to a real original: Old Shoebox Annie, otherwise known as Mrs. Mary Eleanor Smith.

She came from San Francisco and first came to the law's attention by using her small son, Earl, to pass worthless checks. It was a simple system. The boy would go to a store carrying a note and a blank check. The note advised the store staff that the boy was to bring the following items home, then would come the list. The merchant would fill the list, taking the check in payment. He would lose his money when the check bounced, but also quickly lose interest in prosecuting because, "Aw, it was just a kid."

In any case Earl had his instructions. He was to take the blame, all of it, and tearfully sob, "Please don't have me arrested. I forged my mother's name to that check. If she finds out it will kill her."

This was not the lady's maiden voyage into crime. Long ago she had made herself queen of the shoplifters with the unique device from which she got her nickname. Her simple, effective gimmick was nothing more complex than a box without a lid. She would then wrap the box in strong paper and cord, omitting the cord on the unlidded side, and cut a slit in the paper there.

Thus Mary (or Annie, take your choice) had an apparently legitimate purchase, already bought and wrapped; unless somebody was quick enough to see her purloin something and slip it through the slit, she would arouse no suspicion.

By 1914, Earl was all grown up, a thug of vast experience. He had attacked a man for his wallet, beating him viciously until a police officer grabbed him; that got him some reform school time. Once out, he managed to bungle stealing a car and got five years of hard time; his accomplice in the theft went unpunished—dear old Mom.

After he had done his time, he went home to mother, and the two created what they thought was a foolproof plan for murder-for-profit. If nobody can find a body, they reasoned, the government can't prosecute for murder; they were wrong, of course, but the plan seemed so good to them that they built a copper tank beneath the house floor in Anaconda, Montana. This they filled with muriatic acid, which will dissolve nearly anything, and the stage was set. Now they could murder at will, and dissolve the remains; no corpse, no conviction, or so they confidently thought.

They started with a wealthy speculator named Ole Larson, offered him a business deal, and invited him to dinner at their home to discuss the matter. He accepted, and simply disappeared. When the police confronted Earl, he had a ready answer. If I murdered someone, where's the body? Only Earl and his mother knew where the body was, of course: gone to sludge in the trusty acid box.

Next up was an old girlfriend of Earl's, a lady named LaCasse, now wealthy and living in Seattle. They renewed acquaintances, with fatal results for the lady. After she disappeared as well, police followed Earl's trail back to Anaconda. There they found valuables belonging to the vanished woman, including even her monogramed underwear—but no body, of course. The trusty muriatic acid had made Ms. LaCasse disappear altogether.

Earl's sweet mother was once more able to say, "All right, prove we killed her. Find the body." Or words to that effect, again dodging the bullet in spite of their moronic retention of the loot where others could find it. Once again the magic talisman had worked: no corpse, no trouble.

Still, life was a trifle uncomfortable with the police buzzing around, so mother and son moved to Seattle, where Earl turned his hand to stealing cars and selling them. Mama got the lion's share of the proceeds, of course, less sonny boy's allowance. And then, in 1920, the murderous little family reverted to type. This time the victim was a young naval officer, Jim Bassett, who vanished along with his distinctive bright blue roadster. The car turned up—stopped by the police, in fact, with mother and son Smith on board.

Once more the little family's dense approach to crime tripped them up, for the bright blue car held the lieutenant's wallet (empty, of course,) along with his watch and cuff links. That was plenty of evidence for the Seattle police to jail both mother and son for grand larceny. A murder charge would have to wait, for again there was no body. And so dear mother got eight years; sonny went up for life, thanks to his long and fumbling career on the wrong side of the law.

But again the family curse of stupid raised its ugly head. Momma talked when she shouldn't have; momma talked way too much to her prison cellmate, and this is generally what she said: "Well, we did kill Bassett. I already had water boiling in case I needed it to wash up any blood. Earl hit him with a hammer; then we undressed him and dragged him into the bathroom. Earl had big tongs to do things like this, because he was afraid fingerprints might show up on dead bodies."

Tongs? No mental giant, Earl; neither was his mother, as will appear. Next this fragrant pair drained the blood from the body and cut it up in pieces, preparatory to bagging the parts and hauling them into the country for burial by night.

"Then," momma continued matter-of-factly, "we had dinner."

The axe fell just as momma was coming up for parole. Her cellmate was the key the prosecution needed to try the pair for murder, and her testimony was convincing, even delivered above the screams of Annie in the courtroom. Now, all bets were off. Earl, afraid of the death penalty, took his own life in prison. His mother was saved by, of all people, lieutenant Bassett's mother. "I shall be content," she told the court, "if she remains in prison."

And she did, for keeps.

CHAPTER TWENTY

Swindler Extraordinaire

Sophie Lyons

If you're destined to do great things, it helps to be born of promising stock. Sophie Lyons had that advantage: just consider her bloodline. Her father was an accomplished housebreaker, although he was unfortunate enough to spend much of his time in the slammer. One grandfather, back in England, was, as Sophie herself proudly put it, a criminal "to whom Scotland Yard took off its cap."

But the real star of Sophie's world was her mother. That's a normal reaction for a daughter, but momma was different from the usual, being a highly adept shoplifter with at least a couple of aliases.

Sophie was a charming child, who went to school with mom early on, to learn all about life and crime. If you believe Sophie herself, she never went to a real school at all, and only learned to read and write when she was in her twenties. Mom taught her everything else.

Once, the story goes, the child got an idea from some friends that there was something wrong with stealing stuff. Daddy, not in jail at the moment, disabused her of that notion by laying a hot poker along her arm; such notions were foreign to the family business, after all, and she did not forget.

Sophie grew up a beautiful girl, described as having "brilliant dark eyes, and auburn hair that flowed to her feet when shaken from its coils." Much sought-after, she married in her mid-teens to a punk who said he was an expert pickpocket, but soon got caught with his hand in somebody's pocket and went to jail. Sophie closed the books on him forthwith, for in her twisted society and time, criminal expertise was a much-admired attribute.

But wedlock beckoned again, this time to a real man, and a man with real money, too. Although big Ned was also a criminal and a hard man—with one ear bitten off in a brawl—and more than a decade older than Sophie, it seemed a match made in heaven. Ned obviously treasured his young bride, and bought her a Long Island home, stocked it with servants and fine furnishings, and insisted she stay there. No more shop-lifting and other criminal deviltry for her.

But Sophie wasn't having any of it. Although she could wish for no more in care and luxury, the story goes that she could not resist returning to the profession she had practiced from childhood. And so, when Ned was away, Sophie would venture forth to Manhattan and steal whatever looked promising, fence the take herself, and returned home to be the lady of the manor.

Ned seems to have discovered her little hobby, which she continued even after producing a son, George, in 1870. Sophie kept it up, dodging a bullet on one occasion when she was caught picking pockets. This fair young damsel turned on the tears and managed to wriggle out of that one, but she couldn't beat the rap when she was caught scooping up diamond rings in a New York jewelry store. That got her six months.

She parked son George with, of all people, her mother, who would later supervise part of his education in the criminal arts. Either George didn't have the talent or he had no luck at all; he got two long sentences to hard time, and last died in prison. "Cut off in his prime, he was," said Sophie. You have to wonder whether she thought about her part in getting him to travel on that short road.

The next difficulty in Sophie's life was the arrest of her husband, who boosted the wrong safe and got seven years in Sing Sing. Shortly after that Sophie was resident in the woman's side of that ancient prison after a larceny conviction. She quickly became a sort of nursemaid to the warden's kids, even taking them for strolls outside the walls. She soon seized the opportunity to arrange a visit to Ned by his "lawyer," a gang member, who walked out of the prison with his entry pass stuffed in his own mouth.

That pass, duly copied and altered, along with a smuggled wig, got Ned out of prison. And before long he managed to get a pad of wax passed to Sophie—wax she used to make an impression of the door key. Once that was passed to Ned and a key made, it was a piece of cake. Just before Christmas, 1872, Sophie walked out during a heavy snow storm and jumped into a waiting sleigh. Ned welcomed her with a bottle of brandy and a fur coat—stolen, the story goes, just the day before.

The next few years were spent in Canada, and were unexceptional, save for the occasional safe to keep the two in beef and beans. One big job was a pawnbroker's safe that made them richer by $40,000 or so. Now it was Sophie pleading with her husband to go straight, but she had no more luck with him than he had had with her. The two even split up for a little while, but they then tried picking pockets at a fair in 1876 and got caught.

It was back to Sing Sing to finish their sentences, and while she was up the river Sophie decided that Ned was unnecessary; she would go it alone. She had a reputation by this time; she could work with any of several big-time criminal operators. And she was careful. She acquired a new partner, one Billy Burke, and gave him specific cautionary instructions: no shooting, no violence, no blood.

One of her novel ploys involved every American's love of the circus. She made a list of towns in which circuses were to appear, cased a small bank in each town, and then, when the traditional parade drew all the bank's occupants to the front windows, Burke would enter through the back door, rifle the cash drawers, and vanish, with something between $10,000 and $25,000. At this stage of her new career, she kept the bulk of the receipts, while Burke worked for wages.

The next ploy was arriving at a bank in a resplendent carriage, always at the noon hour, when only one teller was on duty. Summoned to speak to the great lady outside, the teller of course went, and while he was gone, Burke, already in the bank as a customer, skimmed the cash drawers.

Sophie even tried Europe, committing burglary and smuggling jewels in the hollow bottom of her trunks. Her masterpiece was the theft of some $500 million in jewelry from a Mrs. Lorillard, who traveled with two maids, one of whom oversaw her two bags of jewelry. Meeting the

Sophie Lyons

maid in the hall on her way to take the bags to the hotel safe, Sophie artfully engaged her in conversation; the girl set down the bags long enough for a confederate to substitute a duplicate bag.

The jewels were taken to another hotel, while Sophie stayed where she was to avert suspicion, even helpfully inviting police investigators to search her room. Even after expenses, Sophie was richer by at least $200,000. For a while, old days and old loves beckoned again, and Ned was back in her life; very much so, three children worth, until at last the bloom was off the rose for keeps and the rocky marriage was finally finished.

But for all her considerable earning power, Sophie was forever in need of money. She turned her hand to blackmail and did quite well at it. One victim, a rich Detroit man, was haunted by the spectacle of Sophie sitting outside his house, playing the woman wronged. And when he at last emerged from his home, he came armed with a hose, with which he knocked the lady down. But there was worse to come.

With the years, Sophie's beauty began to fade, and along the way she acquired an opium habit. Even with that, she remained endlessly inventive. One project was an investment "bank" directed at women, a project that brought in another $200,000 or so. That was a disappointment, however, for a trusted helper departed with all or most of the profit.

But Sophie had discovered a remarkable talent for investment—the real thing—and by the end of the first decade of the twentieth century owned something like forty houses. But Sophie wanted more: "the respect," she said, "of good people."

And but by 1897, Sophie had turned over a new leaf. In an extraordinary role reversal, she became America's first well-known society columnist, writing for the New York *World*. The role was a natural, using all the international contacts she had built up over the years. She now had a villa on the Riviera and traveled back and forth to Europe on the top liners. She wrote about and hobnobbed with the top of society, even, it is said, the Prince of Wales.

On the side she also wrote little "crime-does-not-pay" booklets, urging criminals to reform, to "tread on the past as you would on a doormat." She spent much money on prison libraries and funded a home for children whose parents were in prison. She did her best to personally reform criminals whom she knew. And ironically, tragically, it was three of these that brought down the curtain on one of the most remarkable careers in American history

Three men she had been trying to help had heard all the stories about her hidden booty. And so they invaded her palatial home and pistol-whipped her. When her neighbors heard the commotion and her cries and ran to help, it was already too late. She died in the hospital that night.

Her big safe deposit box was loaded with cash, jewelry, and stocks and bonds, some of it wrapped in an American flag; there was a note attached: "God bless this flag." She was seventy-six.

America is a country of originals; no place else comes even close. But even here, even among the unique peoples of our nation, once in a great while you find somebody about whom you can say, "There'll never be another one like her."

CHAPTER TWENTY-ONE

A Class Act

The Wild Bunch Ladies

Nearly everybody's heard of Butch Cassidy and Harry Longabaugh, better known as the Sundance Kid. Some know about a few of the others, long-time bad men like Kid Curry and the Tall Texan; the whole gang is the subject of dozens of Wild West tales and a legend or two. They were the real thing.

And their ladies? Also the real thing, a good deal more than the average floozy. In their world, the men they ran with were the aristocracy of the land; none of those two-bit grifters and sneak thieves for these women. Many of them started life in the fast lane as prostitutes, of course—maybe most of them. That was the way you met the cream of the outlaw world, for respectable ladies generally didn't hang around saloons, dance halls, and similar dives, the natural habitat of the western tough guy.

There were a couple of other nuclei, too—one the madam of a famous San Antonio bordello, Fanny Porter, the legendary whore with a heart of gold, at least as far as her girls were concerned. She mother-henned them and even granted them extensive furloughs when a long trip with an admirer beckoned. She ran a class outfit, did Fanny, the sort of place the Bunch liked.

Not only were the girls superior—as the Wild Bunch had good reason to know—but Fanny's house was a discreet retreat, a shelter where a man with a price on his head could relax without fear of the law. Texas was their kind of place, welcoming and safely distant from their usual stomping grounds in the Rockies. The man who bought and redeemed

Harry Longabaugh, alias the Sundance Kid, and Etta Place

a token from Fanny's place—marked "good for one"—got his money's worth.

Fanny was also known for her "sampling nights" where, by invitation only, a guest could sample the new girls, free of course—although on those nights whiskey went for outrageously inflated prices. Fanny had a heart of gold, certainly, but she also had an eye for the bottom line.

The other connection was the Bassett family, a unique pioneer clan that were the first to settle near the Green River in Brown's Hole, a fertile refuge out in western Colorado and eastern Utah. Elizabeth Bassett was a dynamic frontier woman, renowned for her knowledge of horseflesh, a breeder of fine horses and a couple of feisty daughters, Ann and Josie, as dynamic as their mother, which is saying quite a lot.

The Bassett ranch always had the welcome mat out for men of the Wild Bunch. While Elizabeth remained always true to her husband, in the apt words of author Michael Rutter, she had "a soft spot in her heart for strays: dogs, cats, cattle, horses and lonely men." And as time went by, so did her daughters. She was given to mothering some of the outlaw fraternity—Butch Cassidy for one—and her solicitude included lots of good advice; she told Cassidy to stop all this outlaw stuff, find a nice girl, and settle down.

So outlaws by and large behaved themselves in Brown's Hole, and part of the herds introduced by rustlers tended to stay in the basin. You couldn't say that Elizabeth and her fellow small ranchers were professional rustlers, but the odd beef—or maybe a lot of them—was welcome to Brown's Hole.

Elizabeth's husband Herb was by contrast a man of books, a teacher, content to take a back seat to his dynamic wife, to read and teach others. He set up and supported the first library for many miles in every direction. Meanwhile, Elizabeth ran the ranch, fed her cowboys well (always a direct route to their hearts), and worked out a system that let her hands share in the profits of roundups and wild cattle drives.

And if in those operations she necessarily collected some cattle not her own, she made sure they got back to their owners, unless, of course, they carried the brand of one of the big, greedy stock corporations, with which all smaller ranchers were at odds. It may well be that some corporation beasts fell into her herd and magically vanished, or so it has been suggested. She had great sympathy for her small-rancher neighbors, but none whatever for the big, faceless corporate competition. As a staunch independent western lady, she followed her own notions of right and wrong.

When the only doctor in the basin passed away, Elizabeth stepped into the breach, supplementing her knowledge of rough frontier medicine with the doctor's medical books, learning as she went along, giving much of her days—and her nights—to healing others. Tough as she was on the outside, her innate kindness continued to shine through, and people of good will could see it.

She was not above some impromptu law enforcement, either, on one occasion tracking down three Texas no-goods who had killed one of her hands. The three ended up decorating trees, and legend tells that Elizabeth adjusted the nooses personally. Given her long and proven dedication to the rancher's profession, she probably did it perfectly, insuring a snapped neck and a quick end.

A memorable lady.

Her daughters were both cut from the same cloth. Both were attractive, bright, determined and well educated. Ann was the younger daughter, but ended up being called Queen of the Rustlers. Her nickname partook of some exaggeration, but she was distinctly her mother's daughter, as disgusted with the big cattle companies as mom ever was. She knew the boys of the Wild Bunch, and as an adult may even have had a romantic fling with Butch Cassidy—it's even been suggested that she was the enigmatic Etta Place, of whom more anon.

She was a special buddy of Elza Lay, Butch's particular sidekick, surely knew Longabaugh, Matt Warner, and Kid Curry, and may even have met Tom McCarty, the outlaw dirtbag who ran from a single citizen-riflemen in little Delta, Colorado, leaving his brother and nephew staring up at nothing in a dusty street.

Ann was a tomboy to the core, who even fought at least once with her sister Josie, an all-out hair-pulling, punch-throwing mini-brawl, but she was also more than willing to take up her mother's battle against the big cattle companies. Even when the big boys had a legitimate legal complaint, or one they could bribe to prosecution, they discovered that juries in the basin were mostly unfriendly, small ranchers and their families.

The corporations at last turned to what seemed to them to be the "final solution," and retained hired killer Tom Horn. Each dead small rancher was worth $500 to Tom, a lot of money for the time, a measure of the devastation the denizens of Brown's Hole were wreaking on the big companies. Seeing a chance to sabotage the enemy from within, Ann even married the manager of the Two Bar Ranch, which she detested above all the other big outfits. It was a union distinctly not made in heaven; it didn't last.

The crisis came when Ann closed down a critical water hole. Without it, the Two Bar could not expand, and so the corporation staged a trial on trumped-up—well, maybe trumped-up—charges of rustling, right down to a fresh hide hanging in her barn. The country rallied 'round her, and sure enough, the jury promptly acquitted her.

Ann got rid of her useless ex-manager and at last married purely for love, a mining man whom she followed as he prospected. Her feisty spirit did not go entirely away. The story goes that during their travels, at a place called Boron, California, she hunted down a mean circus bear, running loose after a train wreck, tracking the beast for several days and finally killing it for the reward.

She was sixty.

Ann died at seventy-eight, still the outdoor woman, still in love with the high country of her birth, distinctly her mother's daughter.

Her elder sister, Josie, was as beautiful as her sibling and her mother, and just as much a tomboy growing up. She could ride and shoot with the best of the men, and she had an eye for the menfolk. She married five of them, not counting a long roster of lovers. Like the rest of her family, she was well educated, attending girls' schools in Boston and Salt Lake City.

She was sweet on Butch Cassidy for a time, and Josie thought that the young outlaw "was the handsomest man I ever seen. I was such a young thing. . . . He was more interested in his horse than he was in me." That lack of feeling did not last, according to legend; the story goes that at a later time Cassidy hid out in the Bassett barn. "Josie," he allegedly said, "I'll get bored all by myself in the hayloft." To which bold Josie replied, "Well, all I can say is, I didn't let him get bored."

Josie also thought a great deal of Bunch member Elza Lay, whom she called "the finest gentleman I've ever known." Whether they were lovers at one time is unclear, but at the least they were good companions. They did share some interest in the outlaw trade—Elza's career is a matter of vivid record; Josie's somewhat lower key.

She was tried for rustling cattle at sixty-two, but was acquitted using the ancient grandmother defense. Duded up in a modest dress, she put on her best innocent face: "I'm a grandma. Do I look like I could rustle cows?" The jury didn't think so, knew her record of local benevolence and/or didn't care. Not guilty.

Besides her casual flirtations with outlaws, Josie continued to marry, sadly without anything approaching lasting success. Her fifth and last legal mate was one Ben Morris, who wasn't a bad sort except when he was in his cups or grumbling about something, which seems to have happened a lot. Things came to a head one day when Ben complained that her gravy was lumpy. Josie, ever the direct pioneer woman, fixed his complaint by dumping the gravy upon him and telling him to "wear it," which perforce he did. She also gave him a quarter of an hour to get lost, and he did that too.

Josie lived out most of the rest of her life on Cub Creek, today part of Utah's Dinosaur National Monument. Deep in her eighties, she lived on in the wild mountain country she loved until she could manage alone no longer. The rest home to which she was moved could not hold her free frontier spirit and she soon passed away.

Of the other Wild Bunch ladies, three stand out. We'll start with the lass known as Etta Place, the heart-throb of Harry Longabaugh, aka the Sundance Kid. She was a slim, elegant lady, who appeared seemingly from nowhere to become his dear companion. We don't know much about her past, whether she had been a prostitute, a shop girl, or somebody's innocent daughter. Maybe she was another of the memorable alums of Fanny's famous establishment in San Antonio. Or not. Even after reams of more-or-less accurate writing, she remains an enigma.

She was what the western boys called a "real looker," a slim woman who wore her dark brown hair pulled up atop her head. The one picture we have of her supports the popular description. She and Sundance may or may not have shared a case of venereal disease—"carnal flu" as it was sometimes called—but they sure shared some high times. Longabaugh even took her to meet his relatives up in Pennsylvania, introducing her as his wife.

Then it was on to New York by way of Niagara Falls. All the way the two demonstrated a taste for the good things of life, fine hotels and the best restaurants. There is no evidence they ever married, but they sure acted like they were.

They met Butch Cassidy in New York and did the town, then sailed for Argentina. That much is certain, but whether she had any active part in the Bunch's crimes either in the United States or South America is unknown. She obviously knew what her beloved did for a living; after all, she helped spend the money. It may even be that she was an accessory, helping out as lookout or horse-holder or in some other way, but if she did we don't know about it for sure. One source even says she held the horses during a 1906 robbery in which a bank president was killed.

Nobody knows for sure even whether Etta came back to the United States with her lover, or indeed whether she came back at all. There are all sorts of tales of her appearances here and there in the United States, among them plying the hooker's ancient profession and then running a brothel in Fort Worth, calling herself Eunice Gray. But there's also a story that she never returned from Argentina, and later married a Paraguayan government official.

And so the story of Etta Place ends as a fascinating tale with huge blank spaces. She remains only an elusive, attractive shadow, and is likely to remain so. Nobody is sure whether she was or was not one of Fanny's illustrious alumnae, but there is evidence that she at least knew Fanny fairly well, maybe as a chambermaid or simply an acquaintance.

There is also an intriguing theory that she and Ann Bassett were one and the same woman. Along the way somebody did a computer analysis of the photos of both women, and concluded that there was only one chance in 5,000 that they were not the same person.

Maybe, maybe not.

And so Etta Place remains an enigma, of all the Wild Bunch women the least well known—but then, mysteries are more fun.

A lot more is known about Laura Bullion, also known as "Rose," "the Thorny Rose," or even "Della Rose." Not nearly as attractive as her sister-in-crime Etta Place, Laura still doubled in brass as mistress to not one but two Wild Bunch members: Ben Kilpatrick (called the Tall Texan) and Will Carver, maybe the toughest and meanest of the Bunch.

Laura was born back in Knickerbocker, Texas, about 1876. Her father got himself killed over in New Mexico trying to rob a train—that was his profession—and things had been tough growing up, since she was on her own early in life. She did some whoring for Fanny Porter in San Antonio and then went north to Wyoming. Maybe she first met the Wild Bunch at Fanny's, maybe not. It is certain, however, that she first took up with the malevolent Carver, but that relationship did not last.

The second try did, with Ben Kilpatrick, the Tall Texan. That seems to have been something of a love match; Laura had the status of a common-law wife, and shared the fortunes, the misfortunes, and the bed of Kilpatrick. She was in fact the only one of the Wild Bunch women who certainly took an active part in one—or more—of the gang's raids.

After Cassidy and Longabaugh had left for safer climes in South America, the Tall Texan pulled a successful robbery in Wagner, Montana, in 1901. He and Laura then embarked on the sort of fine-hotel-top-restaurant grand tour that had become common with the Bunch and their women. They called themselves Mr. and Mrs. Arnold, which may have fooled a series of hotel clerks, but did not buffalo the law. Aliases are certainly advisable when you are trying to avoid the police, but it is also good to stay away from spreading stolen bills everywhere you go. But that is what "Mr. and Mrs. Arnold" did, and the police diligently followed.

Inevitably, the couple's idyll was interrupted by the law, and the honeymoon was over for good. Laura, as one source put it, was "on the point of leaving with $7,000 stuffed in a suitcase." Still not quite thirty, she got five years in prison; once released, she is said to have opened a boarding house—or some less respectable kind of house—and may have waited for Kilpatrick to finish his own sentence. There is no record that they ever met again, however, and Kilpatrick made any future impossible when he tried to hold up a train with a second-rater called Beck.

The Tall Texan bungled the job. Invading the express car went smoothly enough, until an apparently cooperative express agent named Trousdale attracted the veteran bandit's attention to a package on the express car floor. "That's the most valuable part of our cargo," he said, or something like it. But when Kilpatrick bent down to retrieve this prize, Trousdale busted him in the head with a heavy wooden mallet used to provide crushed ice for other valuable cargo: oysters for the better saloons along the line. Exit Kilpatrick. Beck got a bullet from the express car crew just seconds later.

So the Tall Texan got a small patch of ground. What of Laura? Although she was a young woman still, she fades from history.

Which brings us to Rose Morgan, a very different case. While most of the other Wild Bunch women were graduates of Fanny Porter's classy leaping house, Rose seems to have been an ordinary Mormon girl, a respectable, virtuous girl from a ranch near Star Valley in Wyoming.

That was before she met Matt Warner, who had robbed a bank in Telluride, Colorado, with his brother-in-law, the poisonous Tom McCarty, and was hiding out in Star Valley. Now, heretofore Warner had preached repeatedly against anything like permanent involvement with women: love 'em and leave 'em, he said, women don't belong hanging around this business, but then he met Rose and that all changed—in a heartbeat, as it were.

She was by all accounts an exceedingly lovely woman, and a straight shooter, not all that common in the murky world in which the Bunch lived. Warner fell and fell hard.

How much Rose knew about her beloved's dirty business and the large reward on his head is not clear; maybe, at first, absolutely nothing, but as she stayed around him and the rest of the Bunch, she must have realized, and didn't care, at least not enough to leave. Warner was her man, and that was that. There is no evidence that she took an active part in any of the gang's operations, certainly, and perhaps she was content simply to be with her man and hope things turned out for the best.

And in that part of the world where she and Warner met and loved, he was by way of being a respectable man, for the Bunch were always on their good behavior on their home turf; it didn't hurt either that their pockets usually jingled from their last job. He was also a baptized

Laura Bullion, Hole in the Wall gang member

Mormon, which must have reassured Rose and her family. Anyhow, Warner and his cohorts were good citizens, at least in the Basin, so it just may be that Rose did not know much about his real means of making a living.

The two of them left the basin after the first thaw, and along the way ran into Warner's outlaw friend and sometime brother-in-law Tom McCarty, accompanied by a large lady named Sary, whom Warner famously described as "wider than a pony." The foursome made it a double wedding and spent a month-long honeymoon camping near Jackson, Wyoming. Apparently a good time was had by all, and their isolation was good insulation from prowling lawmen.

The next stop was Butte, where both men were able to spend some of their ill-gotten loot on high living with their new wives. But in time the money ran short, and both men had to go back to work. The ladies they stashed in safe, civilized places, while they rode out to replenish the exchequer. In time, of course, the new wives came to realize the nature of the "business" their beloved husbands pursued.

Matt would probably have liked to quit the owlhoot trail, but it appears he didn't know how; his bride urged him to go straight and stay home on the little ranch they had acquired. But the law was still searching, and Matt unlikely to quit anytime soon. And then daughter Hayda arrived in June, and with motherhood Rose at last became demanding. When she could not persuade him to quit the high lonesome and his law-breaking career, Rose at last took Hayda and left Matt.

About this time he promised Rose he'd quit the outlaw ways; she took him back gladly, but although neither of them knew it then, it was too late for them both.

For it was not long afterward that Rose finally sought treatment for a persistent sore on one leg. The "sore" turned out to be cancerous and Rose had to have the leg amputated. Things were aggravated in May, 1896, when Matt had to spend every dime he had to defeat a prosecution (allegedly, some of the cash went to bribe two witnesses). He was acquitted, but they were flat broke and Rose was not getting better.

And then, in June, Rose gave birth to a baby, a boy, but the child did not live long. And then, in September, Matt was convicted of manslaughter and sent away to the Utah State Prison. It was the last straw.

Just a few days later, Rose died of bone cancer. You wonder just a little whether the cancer was not complicated by a hopeless case of a broken heart. Rose deserved better.

Little Rose's tragedy was only a shade less dismal than that of Maud Davis, also a virtuous, attractive Mormon girl. She grew to womanhood up in Utah's Uinta Basin, and there she met a young man helping her brother cut hay in her father's pasture. It didn't take long for love to blossom, but it was a case of Maud loving not wisely, as the saying goes, but too well.

For the young man was Elza Lay, and Maud's brother brought him home to dinner that night. From that time, Maud was hooked by the husky young outlaw with the courteous manners. The fact that he was an outlaw may not have been crystal clear to Maud, and in any case the Wild Bunch members were always on their good behavior in this, their "home country." They were judged by the inhabitants on that conduct; what nefarious things might have gone on elsewhere were little noted nor long remembered by the folks in the Uinta Basin.

Maud also met Butch Cassidy who, like Elza Lay, had also helped out on her father's farm, and, also like Lay, without taking any money for his time and sweat. Whatever stories may have circulated about these men and their friends didn't matter much. Maybe Maud didn't believe the tales about her new love and Cassidy, or just maybe she knew he was on the wrong side of the law for now, but thought he could be reformed.

Maud's parents liked Elza, but were still uneasy about their daughter's obvious infatuation with an outlaw. The fact that Elza was not Mormon was also a concern, but nothing stopped the young couple from marrying. For Maud, the new life was exciting, a heady mix of the high life and living on the edge, hiding out in the outlaw world.

For a while.

In time, however, she got tired of the uncertainty, of life with an absentee husband. Her unhappiness was eased for a while, when Cassidy joined them with a lady of his own; nobody knows any more exactly who the other lady was, but the odds are on the mysterious Etta Place, or maybe Ann Bassett.

Maud's joy increased when she gave birth to a baby girl, a little miracle she called Marvel Lay. But little Marvel's arrival sparked an ultimatum from the new mother: It's time you settled down, she told Elza, it's time to be a family; but it was not to be. It appears that Elza Lay had developed an appetite for danger and life on the edge, and he wasn't about to leave it. The law's search for the Bunch got closer and closer, to the point that it seemed that there was no longer any safe haven.

There wasn't. The hunters of the law ran down Lay at last; he got life in prison over in New Mexico, and Maud at last had had enough and divorced him. In 1899, she tried matrimony again, with a miner named Curry. She had two children by Curry, but her new man shot himself three years after their marriage.

She tried again, with a good man named McDonald, a Canadian rancher with whom she had a child, a son named Ed. It was a happy marriage. Her new husband treated her children from her other marriages as his own, but he died of the flu in the autumn of 1906. Maud tried again in 1912, another successful marriage to photographer Albert Atwood. That union produced a son, and things went smoothly until 1926, when she was notified that her son Albert McDonald, away at school, was gravely ill.

She rushed to his side, but all she could do was nurse him in the last days of a fatal case of pneumonia. Worse, the day he died, she got word that her husband Albert was dying. She got back to him only in time to nurse him in his last hours.

Maud returned at last the Uinta Basin, raising what was left of her own family and extending her boundless sympathy to other people. She became a famous midwife, much admired for helping other people. She lived to be eighty-four years old, and left a glowing memory of love and charity.

Few people remembered her long-ago connection with Elza; or if they did remember, nobody cared. She was quite a lady.

Thus the ladies of the Wild Bunch: good and bad, or a mixture of both. Whatever people thought of them and their choice of men, at the least they were always interesting.

CHAPTER TWENTY-TWO

Just a Pinch of Arsenic

Nannie Doss and Judi Buenoano

Murder by people who kill in anger or fear is not hard for most of us to understand; those emotions are common to most of humankind. What is hard for the ordinary person to fathom is the empty human being, the person to whom other people are simply things, good or bad things, useful things, or simply obstacles.

Those to whom others are simply objects, like a loaf of bread or a park bench, are beyond the power of most of us to understand at all, let alone identify with. They are the hollow people, the empty ones, the men and women who are moved only by self-interest, by what gratifies them, and if another human being interferes with what they want, that person becomes only an annoyance, something to be gotten out of the way.

Nannie Doss came of a hardscrabble farm family, the Hazles, a long way down in Alabama, fathered by a tough bully of a father, put to work early to try to salvage some sort of living from the family farm. Since there wasn't much brightness in Nannie's life, she turned to her dreams; those, like the fantasies of many young girls and women, were of the perfect man. Young Lochinvar would ride in out of the West and sweep them off their feet. They would of course live happily ever after in the arms of their beloved, perhaps in his castle or manor house.

Nannie slept around as a young woman, but the man of her dreams was chosen for her by her father when she was about sixteen. This man, one Charlie Braggs, wasn't quite what Nannie had in mind for her Prince Charming, but the choice wasn't hers to make. She and Charlie were apparently more than compatible in bed—they had four kids—but otherwise Charlie was not the man of her dreams.

He was, in fact, a lush and a philanderer, hardly Mr. Right. Nannie bedded some other men herself, but that hardly made up for the loss of her dream. And so she took action to help her own dream along: Two of her young daughters tragically died in the same afternoon. The doctor said it was food poisoning, but Charlie wasn't so sure; alarmed, he took immediate action, removing both himself and one of his daughters from the area. When he returned, he was with another woman and her child.

So Nannie packed up her two remaining daughters and for a while lived modestly and worked at a mill. And sure enough, in time her dream came true at last. This time it was one Frank Harrelson, who looked like he might be Prince Charming at last. No. Nannie discovered that she had traded in one drunk for another drunk who also like to beat her up and was an ex-con into the bargain.

The miracle was that Nannie put up with it for some sixteen years—almost. For she was once again plagued by deaths in the family, with the tragic demise of her grandchildren while they were in her care. And then it was Frankie-Boy's turn. After a night of protracted sexual fun and games, he expired of acute rat poison, apparently added to his booze stash concealed into the garden.

Two years later, Nannie tried again. This year's Prince Charming was Arlie Lanning, but Arlie lasted only a couple of years and "tragically" passed away. Shortly after that Nannie's house burned down. Homeless, Nannie moved in with Arlie's mother, but his mother died within weeks, of natural causes, of course. Nannie then took refuge with her sister, who died within days.

Nannie didn't seem to be having any luck but bad. But then, in 1952, she met Prince Charming number four, a prominent, retired businessman named Richard Morton. At least he was not a wife beater, but a philanderer he surely was. He was also stone broke, in spite of his respectable appearance. And so, by the spring of 1953, he was also dead, preceded in death by Nannie's own mother, whose exit from this world was accompanied by abdominal pains of unknown origin.

Nannie might have quit at four failed princes, but she took on one more, Sam Doss, who was without the handicaps common to his predecessors, but also without much else. In those days, he would have been called a complete drip, a boring skinflint on his best days, an early-to-bed, early-to-rise serious sort of fellow; none of this modern frivolity for him.

Sam was so much of a straight arrow that he even forbade Nannie the small and innocent frivolity of watching television shows and reading romance magazines. That tore it. The deadly lady prepared a pie delicately seasoned with poison, but the innocent confection only made Sam deadly ill. He returned from the hospital after twenty-three days of treatment and recuperation to be greeted with a succulent roast and a loaded cup of coffee.

Whatever it was, the roast or the coffee, it was deadly. It was also the last hurrah for Nannie, but this time the doctors would not settle for a verdict of death by unknown causes. Instead, they did a thorough autopsy, which turned up enough arsenic in Sam to poison a small army. Nannie was arrested and ultimately confessed after she was promised she could have her romance magazines if she talked.

Nannie, a light-hearted lady in spite of her romantic setbacks, so cheerfully related the details of her extensive poisoning campaign that some question was raised as to her mental stability. An inquiry into her mental condition followed. The result was predictable: She was sane all right; her killing was simply a pragmatic step in aid of eliminating any real or perceived obstacles to her ultimate happiness. In her mind, her four husbands, her children, her mother, her mother-in-law, and some grandchildren were simply impediments to her own happiness, and so they had to go. A pity, of course, but the important thing was herself. She collected some insurance along the way as well, but that was only a secondary benefit.

Freud would have loved her.

Then there was the Black Widow, so-called, Judias Ann Lou Buenoano, who considered killing people as no more than a simple way to make money—your raw materials didn't cost much, and your customers never came back to complain.

Born Judias Wetley in Quanah, Texas in 1943, she had the miserable childhood that so often accompanied growing up in poverty and living on the edge. The family was fractured, too, with Judias and her brother separated from their siblings and hostile to them. They were treated like dirt, burned with cigarettes, until at last Judias lost it at the age of fourteen, attacked her stepmother and father and anointed a couple of her siblings with hot grease. The court gave her a couple of months for that one, plus some reform school time after that—time she is said to have volunteered for, as an alternative to going back to her family.

In 1961 Judias gave birth to a son, Michael, and married an Air Force pilot named James Goodyear. The two events did not occur in the usual order, so it is probable that her offspring had nothing to do her new husband. In any event, the marriage started out well: the couple had two children, and James adopted her son Michael.

But then Judias's idyll fell apart: her pilot husband was assigned to Vietnam, but the couple was lucky; just three months later he came home; but by mid-September, 1971, James Goodyear was dead, cause unknown. Judias collected on his insurance, but then, in less than a year, lost her home to a destructive fire. The insurance on the structure was some comfort, and the family moved to Pensacola.

Some further comfort was Bobby Joe Morris, a new love interest. The couple did not bother marrying, but did some serious cohabiting, including Bobby Joe taking out a policy insuring his own life. In 1977 the couple moved to Trinidad of all places, kids and all. And Bobby Joe died there. He fell suddenly ill and was gone within a month of what was called "cardiac arrest," as undescriptive as a cause of death could be.

Now it was back to Pensacola with the proceeds from Bobby Joe's insurance. The next fatality was son Michael, now nineteen, who had grown up to be a major irritation. He had gotten progressively more and more ill, to the point where he was even partially paralyzed, and when his loving mother took him and a younger sibling for a canoe trip, the canoe somehow tipped over. Judias and her younger son swam to safety, but Michael couldn't swim well and perished.

A terrible domestic tragedy—surely, more than one woman could bear—but her son was, however, insured, so that was some small comfort at least. Some additional comfort came with her new beauty parlor, opened with Michael's insurance, and even more with a new love interest, Pensacola businessman John Gentry.

Judias was getting more and more resourceful. She could provide John with a whole litany of false but pleasant information about herself, including her nursing career and her PhDs in this and that. John fell hard. One of the kind things he did for his new lady was insure himself, but it wasn't long before he began to feel poorly. He declined to the point where he required hospitalization for almost two weeks, but the hospital stay produced a miraculous cure.

It didn't last.

Once home, Judias resumed her tender care for John-Michael, a routine that included his daily dose of vitamin pills. He began to decline again, however, and when his illness began again he began to wonder about those vitamins. He brushed off the thought—love conquers all, even reasonable suspicions—until his car exploded, nearly killing him. Now cars are not usually given to spontaneous explosions. That was enough to overcome even whatever residue of affection still remained, and John-Michael pocketed some of his vitamin pills and went to the police.

Sure enough, those healing little pills were loaded with arsenic, and Judias was in deep trouble: attempted murder of John-Michael and murder of her own son. The police were thorough; they exhumed both Goodyear and Morris and the result came up arsenic again. They were classic cases of murder in the first degree, and the jury agreed. There were the usual appeals—long and drawn out, as appeals are in death penalty cases. But in the end, the conviction stood up. Even so, Judias set a sort of record: In the spring of 1998 she was the first woman to successfully use the Florida electric chair.

CHAPTER TWENTY-THREE

The Shame of Hippocrates

Two Faithless Medics

Most of us trust the medical profession implicitly. They are special people, the healers who take our lives and futures into their hands and wrestle for our health with a variety of ugly diseases and terrible injuries. And by and large these people are more than worthy of our trust and respect.

But once in a while, one of them turns out to be false to the oath of Hippocrates, a monster, a shameful imposter in the healing profession. So it was with "Doctor" Linda Hazzard and "Sister" Amy Archer-Gilligan, as foul a pair of hypocrites as exists in the history of women in crime. First, the doctor.

She ran a "sanitarium" up in Washington state, specializing in a treatment that can only be described as weird, being composed of a combination of consumption of quantities of broth plus enemas that lasted as long as three hours. This bizarre procedure was supposed to be the very thing to deal with "female troubles" and various abdominal pains. Or so the Williamson sisters had heard. They were heiresses to a large Scottish fortune, and had come all the way from Australia to get some magic medical relief from Dr. Hazzard.

In time the good doctor moved both ladies into her new sanitarium, where she could concentrate on her "therapy" and, incidentally, on her real objective: the sisters' money. One sister, Claire, weighing all of fifty pounds, died. Claire had sent a message asking for help from their uncle, John Herbert, but by the time he reached the sisters, it was too late. Dr. Hazzard had covered her trail with all sorts of releases, so the best Mr. Herbert could do was claim Claire's wasted body.

Enter now the sisters' family nurse, Margaret Conway, who quickly got Dora, the other sister, to eat and slowly regain her health. Ms. Conway discovered some of Claire's belongings in the possession of the doctor, and most damning of all, found that the final entry in Claire's diary was a forgery. All of which moved Herbert to contact the British Counsel, who investigated and discovered some new foul thing every time he turned over a rock.

To begin with, he found that there had been over forty deaths of patients under that doctor's tender "care." Dr. Hazzard had signed death certificates showing various causes of death, while other physicians almost uniformly certified causes of her patients' deaths as "starvation." It further appeared that Dr. Hazzard was not a doctor at all, but trained only in nursing.

The newspapers predictably loved all of it, naming the doctor's sanitarium Starvation Heights. The court loved it not at all, and Dr. Hazzard went up the river for manslaughter; the sentence was two to twelve years, and she did eight.

She deserved a great many more.

So did "Sister" Amy Archer Gilligan, who said she was a nurse but couldn't produce a diploma. Nevertheless, Amy did have a gift; people liked and trusted her, and she gradually attracted a loyal following of mostly wealthy people. And for a while her new nursing home prospered. The death rate was unexceptional, and there was no hint of trouble—yet.

But then, in 1907, she moved to a new facility, a modest fourteen-bed rest home in the town of Windsor, Connecticut, which she called the Archer Home for the Elderly and Infirm. There things seemed to go normally, too, at least for a while. Sadly, her husband died in 1910, but there was no hint of irregularity at the time. The home ran as usual, and such deaths as there were, were certified as natural by old Doctor Howard King. She remarried in 1913, a wealthy widower named Michael Gilligan, but further tragedy came to Amy when Gilligan died within a year of their marriage.

As the years went by, however, some relatives of the home's patients began to have second thoughts. The death rate had risen sharply, and there was also the matter of the insurance policies. Each patient was required to put up a premium of $1,000, ostensibly to provide lifetime care and other benefits. The money, it appeared, bought nothing, but ended up in Amy's pockets.

There was much worse to come, in spite of Dr. Howard's regular verdicts of death by natural causes. The heirs of one patient complained to the authorities, who planted a "patient" in the home. He was impressed by the very large quantity of arsenic the home used. "Rats," said Amy, "it's used to kill rats," but the authorities were not impressed, and ordered autopsies of five patients and her husband Michael. All the bodies were loaded with arsenic.

In the end, it developed that Amy had not only poisoned dozens of her rest-home patients but also both her husbands, not even counting the patients she had smothered with their own pillows. She was tried, however, only for a single murder. Old Doctor Howard testified for the defense, of course, even suggesting the preposterous theory that the poison was planted in the victims.

That notion was a non-starter, especially in the face of evidence that in three years the death toll at the small rest home had been forty-eight. The prosecution experts testified that for a home of that size it should have been no more than eight or ten.

And so, Amy ended her days in confinement, first in the state prison, and finally in an asylum. It is not recorded that anybody missed her.

But you wonder what she saw in her dreams.

CHAPTER TWENTY-FOUR

The Modest Ambition of Jane Toppan

The world saw the last of Jane Toppan in 1938, and a good thing it was, too. For early in her lifetime Jane was well on her way to reaching her ambition, simply to "have killed more people—helpless people—than any other man or woman who ever lived."

That's the way she was quoted anyway, and given her bravura performance as a multiple murderess, that may well have been her heart's desire. That she didn't quite reach her goal sure wasn't for lack of trying.

Jane was the daughter of Irish immigrants, a girl whose portrait radiates a pleasant, dignified and harmless nature. She was born Honora Kelley, and her picture looks like what a good Irish girl ought to be. Maybe it was taken on one of her good days, but her nature was something else entirely.

Maybe the death of her mother when Jane was only a small child had something to do with what Jane was or became, especially since her father, tailor Paul Kelley, was very little help.

He is said to have been passing strange himself, known to other people as Kelley the Crack; crack, that is, as in crackpot. One story about him tells of someone finding him busily engaged in trying to sew his own eyelids shut, some hint of the chaos inside what passed for his brain.

One thing he did right. When Honora was only six, and her older sister Delia but eight, he walked them into the Boston Female Asylum, a shelter or orphanage for indigent kids. There he simply dumped them and walked away, never to return. The home recorded, no doubt accurately, that the two little sisters were "rescued from a very miserable home." There seems to be little question about that.

Little Honora remained in the orphanage only two years or so, for in the autumn of 1864 she was farmed out as an indentured servant in

Lowell, Massachusetts. Her new mistress, Ann Toppan, seems to have treated the little girl well: there was no formal adoption, but thereafter Honora Kelly became Jane Toppan for all time. At least one source says she was adopted by the Toppan family straight from the orphanage. Whatever the case, she became a Toppan child.

Jane bloomed in her new family. She was a good student, and popular with the young men in the community as she grew up. And in time she became engaged to one of the local boys, Jane proudly wearing a ring with a bird carved on it. At least until her light o'love, out of town job hunting, dropped her a short note just to let her know he'd married somebody else.

Jane was crushed, smashed the ring into junk, and never thereafter—or so the story goes—was able to talk about birds or even look at their pictures. Jane withdrew into herself and turned to the seer business, studying dreams until she was sure she could see into the future. When she found out it didn't work, she tried suicide. That didn't work either.

In 1885, presumably the beneficiary of Mrs. Toppan's goodness, Jane entered nurse's training at Cambridge Hospital. She did well, "the most popular nurse in the hospital," a hard and willing worker. According to one source, she was generally known as "Jolly Jane." Her twisted personality had by now appeared, but only at times when she was alone and unobserved except by very ill patients. She liked to experiment, it seems, with seeing what effect varying doses of atropine and morphine would produce in patients under her care. She falsified the patients' charts, of course, carefully covering her tracks as they slid in and out of consciousness.

Jane spent all the time she could spare alone with her selected patients, even climbing into bed with some of them, going so far as to hold them while they died. Whether any sexual doings were involved is unknown, although something she said much later casts a distinct sexual shadow over her "experiments."

Jane admitted that she got a sexual rush out of her selected patients as they slipped into death, revived, and then finally passed away. None of these extracurricular activities were discovered during her years at Cambridge; in fact, she was recommended for further service at highly regarded Massachusetts General Hospital. This was new ground, but Jane went on ploughing it in the same old way. Several more of her patients shuffled off this mortal coil before she got herself fired in 1890, allegedly after a question and answer session in the office of the chief surgeon.

Jane returned to Cambridge briefly, but got herself discharged there, too. The charge was something to do with careless prescription of opiates; or maybe it was because she had never become a graduate nurse—although she had a diploma, it turned out to be forged.

Any chance that this latest firing would save the lives of innocent patients vanished when Jane turned her hand to a new career as a private nurse. It was an occupation made for an empty, evil person: no overseer, no head nurse, nobody to protect her patients from her vile little experiments. She made the most of it. "I will go to the old and the sick," said she, "to comfort them in their neediest hour."

She is quoted as saying precisely that, but the "comfort" she really had in mind had nothing to do with her sick and aged patients. Instead, Jane was bound to heal herself, either cure or feed an eerie, ugly passion that drove her deeper and deeper into evil.

Once begun as a private nurse, Jane had to weather complaints that she engaged in petty thievery, but those were easy enough to evade; you just moved on to another job. Now she could get down to work in earnest. She started close to home by murdering her landlords in 1895; then, as far as the records show, apparently took a break until 1899, when she fed her foster sister Elizabeth a mortal ration of strychnine.

In 1901 she joined the Alden Davis household in Cataumet, Massachusetts. Mrs. Mattie Davis had recently passed away—Jane was certainly positive of that; after all, she had murdered the lady herself. Mattie was an old family friend, and had visited Jane while she was still in Cambridge. But during that visit Mattie had contracted a very sudden, very severe illness; in spite of nursing by Jane, Mattie had passed away, and Jane brought her body home to Cataumet. Mattie's family was of course grateful.

In a matter of just weeks, Alden was dead of some mysterious illness, and with him two of his daughters. What Jane hoped to gain is not clear, maybe the hand of elderly Alden Davis, but whatever her notion was, the scheme never came to fruition. Maybe Jane was just indulging her passion for killing people, for in a remarkably short time both Davis and his two married daughters succumbed to whatever mysterious, enervating disease had been bothering them.

In the past, Jane had managed to get away with her deadly plots, but this time would be different. For one thing, Jane had blocked an autopsy on one of the murdered daughters. Autopsies were contrary to the "religious beliefs" of the Davis family, she said; and there was more damaging evidence. Another relative, Beulah Jacobs, coming in just too late to save Mrs. Gibbs, the last Davis daughter, added more alarming news. Mrs. Gibb's husband, also a ship captain and just home from the sea, learned from Beulah Jacobs that "your wife tried to talk but she couldn't, and she acted scared every time Nurse Toppan came near her." That, coupled with the news of the blocked autopsy, was a red flag to the captain, and he went to the police.

This time there was an autopsy by a competent chemist, who pronounced that Mrs. Gibbs had died of morphine poisoning. An officer set out to the home of Jane's foster mother, only to learn there had been still another death. This time it was Jane's foster sister, who had been feeling poorly and was given a "tonic" prepared by Jane. The detective was too late to save her.

But he was in time to stop still another killing. Even then, Jane was on another private nursing job up in New Hampshire, where one George Nichols had retained her to care for his ailing sister. The detective reached the brother's house to find Jane laughing, "her glowing eyes traveling from sister to brother." Then and there he arrested her. The police and prosecutors knew by now that they were dealing with a lady who was probably playing with something well short of a full deck.

Jane had much public support because of her family name. Several families with social names donated to a defense fund for her, but the police investigation turned up bodies by the dozen, former patients of the respected Nurse Toppan, all the of the bodies full of morphine and atropine. And at last they found the source of Jane's raw material, a pharmacist who dispensed enormous quantities of morphine to her. They were all on prescription, he said—and so they were, but the prescriptions were excellent forgeries, all done by Jane herself.

Jane went from denying the charges against her to exultant admission, boasting of her cleverness in getting away with murder—literally.

Once her confession hit the paper, Back Bay support dwindled away, and what remained of the fat defense fund was returned to the donors.

The toll of Jane's victims may well have been substantially more than the thirty-one Jane admitted. One estimate runs to more than twice that figure, and considering the amount of time Jane had to work, and the number of credulous subjects she had to work with, the roster of the dead may be even longer.

It developed that she used morphine as her primary tool, and then used atropine to re-expand the victim's pupils, counteracting the tell-tale signs of morphine poisoning. And she talked at length and in detail about her killings, which often took days or weeks to complete. As a sort of gruesome finale to her grim admissions, she told a psychiatrist, "I want to go on and on. I want to be known as the greatest criminal that ever lived. That is my ambition!"

When the case came on for trial in June of 1902, Jane entered a plea of "Not Guilty by Reason of Insanity." There was ample evidence of insanity, of Jane's rambling comments, things like "I had to do it. It relieved me." The press remarked on her calm demeanor, on her "laughing and joking" with her counsel, but also reported her violent outburst at the psychiatric testimony.

"The alienist lies!" she shouted, "I am not crazy! . . . I understand right from wrong!" and some more of the same. On the basis of the clear evidence of insanity in her father and one of her sisters, and the very nature of her bizarre case, she was accordingly found not guilty, and forthwith committed for life to the Taunton Insane Hospital.

It was probably there that Jane gave her own estimate of her murdered victims. It was over a hundred, she said. Some of them, like the ones she committed in her student nurse days, she casually called "practice murders."

As time dragged on in the asylum, Jane became more and more paranoid, to the point that she was convinced that "many attempts" were made to kill her. She wrote her doctor to that effect at least once, and in a letter to her sister confided that "a supervisor put some poison in my tea."

She never came out of the asylum until her death at eighty-four, which was probably a very good thing for the world outside. After her death in the summer of 1938, nurses told stories to the press about Jane's periodic smiling invitations to nurses, "Get some morphine, dearie, and we'll go out in the ward. You and I will have a lot of fun seeing them die."

After Jane's death, one of the doctors commented on the institution's prize patient. "She never gave us any trouble. She was just a quiet old lady."

Doctor, you should have seen her back when . . .

CHAPTER TWENTY-FIVE

The Gentle Ladies of New York

The Big Apple can—and does—lay claim to being the most glamorous city in the western hemisphere, sophisticated, urbane, a center of civilized society, theatre, opera, and music. There are lots of beautiful people about, especially in Manhattan. It has its darker side, of course, like any other metropolitan center anywhere, garden variety murder, robbery, arson, rape—the usual thing, *blasé* New Yorkers would say.

But once upon a time, back in the early to mid-nineteenth century, New York had another, notorious side. Those were the days of the great gangs, the Dead Rabbits, the Shirt Tails, the aptly named Forty Thieves, the Bowery Boys, the Plug Uglies, the Charlton Street Gang, the Gophers, the Pansies, to name some of the most famous. They changed names from time to time: the Dead Rabbits, for instance, had once been part of the Roach Guards, and were also called the Blackbirds.

They wore some sort of distinguishing mark, a stripe of some distinctive color, a derby hat. The Dead Rabbits are said to have carried the corpse of a defunct bunny into battle, impaled on some sort of spear. And of course the gangs all owned, or tried to own their own turf, which was to be defended against all comers. The members rejoiced in a variety of colorful names, memorable handles like Cow-legged Sam and Slobbery Jim. One murdered luminary called "Bill the Butcher," for example, was described in an 1855 issue of the Brooklyn Eagle, as a "rum shop rowdy; a knock-down, gouging, biting, brutal savage, whose end is quite in accordance with his previous life."

This collection of vicious hoodlums haunted the Bowery, Hell's Kitchen, and Five Points, dirty, overcrowded, stinking slums. The Charlton Street Gang worked the Hudson River docks, even though these were somewhat better lighted and what security there was, was more alert. The gang made it work for them, however, and one tale tells that they even expanded into piracy along the river, boarding unsuspecting ships and lighters and looting them. They also invaded homes and warehouses along the river, and are said to have held citizens for ransom as a sidelight.

The other major gangs tended to concentrate their activities along the darker, less secure East River docks and their adjacent flophouses and low-life bars, preying on sailors and stealing merchandise from the piers. Inevitably, the gangs' enterprise led to turf wars. Their members engaged in real pitched battles for turf, for pride and political influence, for at least the major gangs hired on to support rival political parties. Irish influence was strong around Five Points, and Irish gangs sometimes banded together to fight pitched battles with "native-born" gangs.

These fracases were no gentle shoving matches. A fallen gang member had a very good chance of being beaten to death, and broken bones, smashed faces, and deep slashes were quite common. The combatants bloodied each other with paving stones, clubs, knives, axes, and even firearms, and for at least a while the police prudently stayed out of these brawls. Except, that is, for some of the political battles, in which rival gangs were joined by rival police forces. One such massive fight took place on the 4th of July, 1857, pitting the Municipal Police (locally run) against the Metropolitan Police (state run), together with an array of allied gangs.

The gangs were a sort of equal-opportunity employer, too; they included some of the most unpleasant, uncivilized, unfeminine women ever to walk on the wild side. The ladies—if that's an appropriate word— of course served male gang members as what the World War II Japanese forces politely called "comfort women," but some were more than that—a lot more, like a harridan called Battle Annie, who led the female warriors of the Gopher gang. Three of them will illustrate what holy terrors some of the gentler sex became.

Sadie the Goat, for instance, won her name from her endearing habit of headbutting people she didn't like, starting with men she was setting up for her boyfriend to rob. It was also a handy method of settling disputes with other gangland harridans. Sadie is said to have played a major role in the gang's depredations, even rising to command a small pirate boat. This tale is embroidered by stories of making people walk the plank and flying the Jolly Roger.

Some of these tales strain credulity, so some, maybe much, of her resume may be invention. Great old tales tend to get greater and more detailed with time, but Sadie the Goat was surely the real McCoy.

One thing seems certain, because Sadie was the living proof. She had only one ear, which made her somewhat lop-sided, at least. The missing ear had fallen to the deadly teeth of one Gallus Mag, a very tough Englishwoman well over six feet tall. She and Sadie got into a fight—almost inevitable, given the temperament of the two—and Mag's teeth were sharper than Sadie's ear. Mag kept the ear and pickled it in a jar at her place of business, a treasured souvenir, pickled along with other mementos of her violent days.

Gallus Mag was not a good person to tangle with, given her size—monstrous for the time—and her occupation: she was a bouncer by trade, in a very bad saloon called The Hole in the Wall, a joint down on Water Street. Mag apparently had a favorite technique with obstreperous customers. She carried a club, and having bashed the peace disturber with it, she would then stand the victim up, seize him by one ear with her teeth, and march him out the door. The other patrons are said to have much enjoyed this miniature floor show, especially when the unfortunate evictee objected, for then the next step was for Mag to bite his ear off as she had promised him she would if he didn't behave.

Mag took pride in her work, and carefully preserved her victims' ears in a jar of alcohol that sat chastely behind the bar. It was her tiny trophy case, and perhaps served, as the French say, "to encourage the others." She did have her sentimental side, according to one story, as when she made peace with her erstwhile enemy, Sadie the Goat. That tale tells that Sadie approached Mag, seeking peace and reconciliation. Mag was so touched that she not only accepted, but graciously returned Sadie's ear.

This formidable woman could well lay claim to being the queen of tough, but there were other claimants in the hard world of the New York waterfront. One of these was a lady who rejoiced in the title of Hellcat Maggie, who may just have been even tougher. Maggie was everybody's worst nightmare, especially when she was girded for war. Not content with conventional weaponry, Maggie filed her teeth to sharp points, and donned sets of metal claws that fit over her hands and fingers. If she didn't bite great chunks out of her opponents, she raked their faces and bodies; a nasty piece of work indeed.

Maggie belonged to the gang called the Whyos, said to have been so named because their recognition signal sounded something like a bird call—well, that's the story, anyhow. Maggie was a "shoulder-hitter," a term apparently equivalent to the "enforcer" of later times.

Thus the women of the New York gangs: very tough, very violent, very colorful indeed. Not somebody you'd take home to dinner or want to introduce to your maiden aunt.

But never dull.

AFTERWORD

This little book has only scratched the surface of the history of American women who walked on the Dark Side, either following men who were professional criminals or themselves breaking the rules that glue society together. There are many other similar stories, areas in which this book has only provided a glimpse of the showy, loud, glamorous world of the mob moll.

And there is the world of espionage, the shadow world of the spy, national and international, the world of Mata Hari and her sisters. Maybe the chance will come to explore the murky land in which these ladies lived—and sometimes died.

Maybe I'll write another volume.

BIBLIOGRAPHY

Baker, Pearl. *The Wild Bunch at Robbers Roost*. Lincoln, NE: University of Nebraska Press, 1971.

Barrow, Blanche, and John Neal Phillips. *My Life with Bonnie and Clyde*. Norman: University of Oklahoma Press, 2004.

Bollinger, Jordan. *Sisterly Love*. Castaic, CA: Desert Breeze Publishing Co., 2013.

Brant, Marley. *The Outlaw Youngers*. Lanham, MD: Madison Books, 1992.

Chapman, Hazel. *Coffeyville Journal*. Skiatook: Oklahoma, October 2, 1991.

Coleman, Jane Candia. *I, Pearl Hart*. Unity, ME: Five Star, 1998.

Cunningham, Eugene. *Triggernometry*. Caldwell, ID: Caxton Printers, 1989.

Dalton, Emmett. *Beyond the Law*. Coffeyville, KS: Coffeyville Historical Society, 1992.

———. *When the Daltons Rode*. Garden City, NY: Doubleday, Doran & Co., 1931.

Drago, Harry Sinclair. *Notorious Ladies of the Frontier*. New York: Dodd, Mead & Co., 1969.

———. *Road Agents and Train Robbers*. New York: Dodd, Mead & Co., 1973.

Edge, L. L. *Run the Cat Roads*. New York: Dembner Books, 1981.

Enss, Chris. *Bedside Book of Bad Girls*. Helena, MT: Farcountry Press, 2012.

Erdoes, Richard. *Saloons of the Old West*. New York: Gramercy Press, 1979.

Ernst, Robert B. *Robbin' Banks and Killin' Cops*. Baltimore, MD: PublishAmerica, 2009.

Garrett, Pat F. *The Authentic Life of Billy the Kid*. New York: Indian Head Books, 1994.

Geary, Rick. *The Saga of the Bloody Benders*. New York: Nantier, Beall, Minoustchine, 2007.

Girardin, G. Russell, and William J. Helmer. *Dillinger: The Untold Story.* Bloomington: Indiana University Press, 2008.

Guinn, Jeff. *Go Down Together.* New York: Simon & Schuster, 2009.

Hamilton, Stanley. *Machine Gun Kelly's Last Stand.* Lawrence: University of Kansas Press, 2003.

Hardy, Allison. *Kate Bender, the Kansas Murderess: The Horrible History of an Arch Killer.* Girard, KS: Haldeman-Julius, 1944.

Harman, S. W. *Hell on the Border.* Lincoln, NE: Bison Books, 1992.

Helmer, William J., and Rick Mattix. *The Complete Public Enemy Almanac.* Nashville, TN: Cumberland House, 2007.

Horan, James. *Desperate Women.* New York: Putnam, 1952.

Hornberger, Francine. *Mistresses of Mayhem.* Indianapolis, IN: Alpha, 2002.

Indian-Pioneer Papers, interview with Elsie Brook, July 12, 1937.

Jahns, Pat. *The Frontier World of Doc Holliday.* New York: Indian Head Books, 1957.

James, John T. *The Benders in Kansas.* Mostly Books: Pittsburg, KS: Mostly Books, 1995.

Jessen, Ken. *Colorado Gunsmoke.* Loveland, CO: J.V. Publications., 1986.

Jones, Richard Glyn (ed). *Women Who Kill.* New York: Carroll & Graf, 2002.

Kansas City Star, May 10, 1931.

Kelly, Charles. *Butch Cassidy and the Wild Bunch.* New York: Konecky & Konecky, 1938.

King, Jeffery S. *The Life and Death of Pretty Boy Floyd.* Kent, OH: Kent University Press, 1998.

Kingston, Charles. *Remarkable Rogues: The Careers of Some Notable Criminals of Europe and America.* Ann Arbor: University of Michigan, 1921.

Los Angeles Evening Herald and Express, October 7, 1935.

Metz, Leon Claire. *The Shooters.* El Paso, TX: Mangan Books, 1976.

Miller, Nyle H. and Joseph W. Snell. *Great Gunfighters of the Kansas Cowtowns.* Lincoln: University of Nebraska Press, 1967.

Miller, Ronald Dean. *Shady Ladies of the West.* Los Angeles: Westernlore Press, 1964.

Morgan, R. D. *Bad Boys of the Cookson Hills.* Stillwater, OK: New Forums Press, 2002.

———. *Bandit Kings of the Cookson Hills.* Stillwater, OK: New Forums Press, 2011.

———. *The Tri-State Terror: The Life and Times of Wilbur Underhill.* Stillwater, OK: New Forums Press, 2011.

Nash, Jay Robert. *Encyclopedia of Western Lawmen and Outlaws.* New York: DaCapo Press, 1994.

———. *Look for the Woman.* New York: M. Evans & Co., 1981.

———. *Hustlers and Conmen.* New York: M. Evans & Co., 1976.

Neal, Bill. *Getting Away with Murder on the Texas Frontier.* Lubbock: Texas Tech University Press, 2006.

O'Neal, Bill. *Encyclopedia of Western Gunfighters.* Norman: University of Oklahoma Press, 1979.

Palmer, Hollis A. *Curse of the Veiled Murderess.* Saratoga Springs, NY: Deep Roots Publications, 2004.

Phillips, John Neal. *Running with Bonnie and Clyde.* Norman: University of Oklahoma Press, 1996.

Poulsen, Ellen. *Don't Call Us Molls.* New York: Clinton Cook Publishing Co., 2002.

Rutter, Michael. *Bad Girls.* Helena, MT: Farcountry Press, 2008.

Samuelson, Nancy B. *The Dalton Gang Story: Lawmen to Outlaws.* Little Rock, AR: Shooting Star Press, 1992.

Sandwich, Brian. *The Great Western.* El Paso: University of Texas El Paso, 1991.

Seagraves, Anne. *Soiled Doves.* Hayden, ID: Wesanne Publications, 1994.

Shirley, Glenn. *Belle Starr and Her Times.* Norman: University of Oklahoma Press, 1972.

———. *Gunfight at Ingalls.* Stillwater, OK: Barbed Wire Press, 1990.

———. *West of Hell's Fringe.* Norman: University of Oklahoma Press, 1978.

Smith, Robert Barr. *Daltons!* Norman: University of Oklahoma Press, 1996.

———. *Last Hurrah of the James Younger Gang.* Norman: University of Oklahoma Press, 2001.

———. *Outlaw Tales of Oklahoma.* Guilford, CT: Globe Pequot Press, 2008.

———. *Tough Towns.* Guilford, CT: Globe Pequot Press, 2007.

Swierczyknski, Duane. *This Here's a Stickup*. Indianapolis, IN: Alpha, 2002.

Tippet, Pam Paden. *Run Rabbit Run: The Life, the Legend, and the Legacy of Edna "Rabbit" Murray, "The Kissing Bandit."* CreateSpace, 2013.

Wilson, Colin, World *Famous Crimes*. New York: Carroll & Graf, 1995.

Wilson, David. *Henrietta Robinson*. New York: Miller, Orton & Mulligan, 1955.

Wilson, R. Michael. *Encyclopedia of Stagecoach Robbery in Arizona*. Las Vegas: Rama Press, 2003.

Winters, Robert. *Mean Men:The Sons of Ma Barker*. Danbury, CT: Rutledge Books., 2000.

Wood, Fern Morrow. *The Benders*. Chelsea, MI: BookCrafters, 1992.

Yadon, Lawrence J., and Robert Barr Smith. *Old West Swindlers*. Gretna, LA: Pelican Press, 2011.

———. *One Murder Too Many*. Gretna, LA: Pelican Press, 2014.

INDEX

About the Author

Robert Barr Smith entered the United States Army as a private in 1958. He served in Vietnam with the 4th Infantry Division, more than seven years in Germany, and with troop units and on posts throughout the United States, retiring as a Colonel. He is a Senior Parachutist, and holds the Legion of Merit (two awards), the Bronze Star, and other decorations.

He holds two degrees from Stanford University and is a Professor of Law Emeritus at the University of Oklahoma, where he also served six years as Associate Dean for Academics and Associate Director of the Law Center. He lives in the Ozark Hills of southern Missouri, and is the author or coauthor of sixteen books and more than a hundred magazine articles, primarily in military and western history.